200 pasta dishes

hamlyn | all colour cookbook

200 pasta dishes

Maria Ricci

An Hachette Livre UK company

First published in Great Britain in 2008 by Hamlyn,
a division of Octopus Publishing Group Ltd
2–4 Heron Quays, London E14 4JP
www.octopusbooks.co.uk

Copyright © Octopus Publishing Group Ltd 2008

Some of the recipes in this book have previously appeared
in other books published by Hamlyn.

ISBN: 978-0-600-61727-3

A CIP catalogue record for this book is available from the
British Library

Printed and bound in China

1 2 3 4 5 6 7 8 9 10

Both metric and imperial measurements have been given
in all recipes. Use one set of measurements only, and not
a mixture of both.

Standard level spoon measurements are used in all recipes.
1 tablespoon = one 15 ml spoon
1 teaspoon = one 5 ml spoon

Ovens should be preheated to the specified temperature
– if using a fan-assisted oven, follow the manufacturer's
instructions for adjusting the time and the temperature.

Fresh herbs should be used unless otherwise stated.

Medium eggs should be used unless otherwise stated.

The Department of Health advises that eggs should not be
consumed raw. This book contains some dishes made with
raw or lightly cooked eggs. It is prudent for vulnerable
people such as pregnant and nursing mothers, invalids, the
elderly, babies and young children to avoid uncooked or
lightly cooked dishes made with eggs. Once prepared, these
dishes should be kept refrigerated and used promptly.

This book includes dishes made with nuts and nut
derivatives. It is advisable for those with known allergic
reactions to nuts and nut derivatives and those who may be
potentially vulnerable to these allergies, such as pregnant and
nursing mothers, invalids, the elderly, babies and children, to
avoid dishes made with nuts and nut oils. It is also prudent to
check the labels of pre-prepared ingredients for the possible
inclusion of nut derivatives.

contents

introduction

introduction

Pasta might be a traditionally Italian dish but it's not surprising that people all around the world have embraced it as a firm favourite, often eating pasta one or more times a week. Pasta is the ultimate convenience food: quick and easy to prepare, extremely versatile due to the numerous pasta shapes and sauce combinations possible and suitable for any occasion, be it a weekday meal or a sophisticated dinner party.

fresh pasta versus dried

People often have the misconception that fresh pasta is superior or somehow more sophisticated than dried. This couldn't be further from the truth. Fresh pasta is reserved for specific shapes and sauces, and is most frequently eaten in central and northern Italy.

In certain regions of southern Italy, such as Sicily, people who eat pasta every day might never even have tasted it fresh! Unless otherwise specified, the recipes in this book use dried pasta. However, where bought filled pasta is required, always use the fresh variety.

Buying fresh pasta from a supermarket can lead to disappointing results. Gluey texture and blandness are all too common, so take the time to search out a good Italian deli, where the pasta is made daily and the best ingredients are used for the job. You'll find a recipe for traditional flour-and-egg-based pasta dough on page 10 and the final chapter in the book (see pages 216–235) is dedicated entirely to homemade pasta recipes.

Dried pasta can be made with or without egg, using durum wheat and/or soft wheat flour. The choice of shapes and brands can be mind-boggling, so below is a useful guide to what shapes to choose for different sauces. When it comes to brands, it is best to go for Italian. These products are widely available, and the ingredients and expertise that go into their production make them far superior to most supermarket brands.

matching pasta shapes & sauces

Italians have strong opinions regarding the pastas that should be used with different sauces, and any general rule that tries to define the criteria to use when making your choice will invariably be compromised by a long list of exceptions. Ultimately, the best combination is the one that works for you, but the following suggestions can help you make an informed choice.

chunky sauces

The hollow pasta shapes with ridges, such as conchiglie, penne, rigatoni or garganelli, or the twisted pastas, such as fusilli, are all ideal for catching tasty chunks. Alternatively, you can opt for one of the long, egg-based pastas, such as pappardelle, tagliatelle or fettuccine. The inclusion of egg makes the pasta more absorbent and this, together with the wide surface of these types of pasta, encourages the sauce to cling to the pasta. Chunky sauces tend just to slide off thin, long strands, such as spaghetti – that's why a true Italian would never serve an authentic Bolognese sauce with spaghetti!

creamy & buttery sauces

For the same reasons mentioned above, egg pasta is the perfect partner for cream- or butter-based sauces. However, these sauces are incredibly versatile and will also happily cling to most short pasta shapes, such as farfalle, fusilli or penne.

oil-based sauces

This is where long, thin dried durum wheat pasta, such as spaghetti or linguine, come into their own. They're ideal for tomato, fish or vegetable sauces that use olive oil as their base ingredient. These pastas won't absorb the oil (as egg pasta would), but instead get a lovely, silky coating of glistening sauce.

perfect cooking

By following these few simple guidelines, you can ensure that your pasta is cooked to perfection, every time.

plenty of salted boiling water

Cook your pasta in a very large saucepan, full of boiling water. This will give it plenty of space to expand into as it cooks and the movement created by the rolling boil will keep it from sticking. Giving the pasta a quick stir halfway through cooking will also help to keep the shapes or strands separate. You'll need enough salt in the water to ensure that the cooked pasta does not taste bland, even before you add the sauce.

al dente

We've all heard this Italian expression for knowing when pasta is cooked, but if it's never been explained clearly, it's hard to know what to aim for. *Al dente* literally translates from the Italian as 'to the tooth', meaning that when you bite into the pasta, it should give on the outside but still retain a little bite in the centre. However, it should be cooked all the way through, with no raw, dry white pasta visible in the centre.

dressing the pasta

Italians always serve their pasta already coated in sauce, as opposed to having a plate of plain pasta with a spoonful of sauce over it. This ensures that all the pasta is well coated in just the right amount of sauce for that particular dish. Many of the recipes in the book instruct you to reserve some of the cooking water from the pasta, combine the drained pasta with its sauce over heat, then add some of the reserved cooking water. This might seem odd at first, but there is a simple explanation. Italians only use enough sauce to lightly coat their pasta. Adding the starchy cooking water and stirring it over the heat encourages the sauce to cling better to the pasta, giving it a rich, silky quality that it wouldn't otherwise achieve.

making pasta

You shouldn't think of making your own pasta as a daunting task. In fact, it's much less prone to disaster than pastry making. You will, however, need some practice to become completely comfortable with the process, so avoid making pasta for the first time when you are expecting important guests!

basic pasta dough

The recipes in this book call for a 1-, 2- or 3-egg quantity of pasta. Make sure that you check the quantity needed before starting.

1-egg pasta dough
Makes **about 150 g (5 oz)**
75 g (3 oz) **Italian 00 flour** or **fine plain flour**, plus extra for dusting
25 g (1 oz) **semola di grano duro**, plus extra for dusting
1 **egg**

2-egg pasta dough
Makes **about 300 g (10 oz)**
 150 g (5 oz) **Italian 00 flour** or **fine plain flour**, plus extra for dusting
50 g (2 oz) **semola di grano duro**, plus extra for dusting
2 **eggs**

3-egg pasta dough
Makes **about 400 g (13 oz)**
225 g (7½ oz) **Italian 00 flour** or **fine plain flour**, plus extra for dusting
75 g (3 oz) **semola di grano duro**, plus extra for dusting
3 **eggs**

Combine the flour and semola in a large bowl. Make a well in the centre and break in the eggs. Mix in the eggs with your fingers, slowly drawing in the flour as you go. Once the central mixture becomes too thick to handle, use the heel of your hand and knead to bring the mixture together. Alternatively, put all the ingredients in a food processor and pulse until combined.

Tip the dough on to a clean work surface dusted with Italian 00 or fine plain flour and knead for 3–4 minutes until it becomes smooth and elastic. Wrap in clingfilm and chill for at least 30 minutes, or up to 4 hours.

rolling out

Dust your work surface with Italian 00 or fine plain flour. Set up a pasta machine at the largest opening. Cut the pasta dough into lemon-sized pieces and pick up one piece, keeping the remaining dough covered with clingfilm. Shape the dough you're holding roughly into a rectangle and run it through the machine. Fold the dough in half widthways and then run it through the machine again. Lower the setting on the machine by one notch and run the dough through it again.

Continue running the dough once through each setting until you have gone through all the settings. If while you're working you find that the pasta sheet is getting too long to handle, cut it in half and run one half through at a time. If it becomes sticky and catches in the pasta machine, dust with a little Italian 00 or fine plain flour.

Lay the pasta sheet on a surface dusted with semola, then cover with a tea towel while you roll out the remaining dough.

Don't waste any time when shaping your rolled-out pasta – the dough will dry incredibly quickly, so work with all speed while it's still moist and pliable.

cutting pasta shapes

Don't worry about taking out your ruler – lasagne sheets can be cut out to suit the size of your baking dish. You can use a large, sharp knife or a crinkle cutter.

To turn your pasta sheets into pappardelle, tagliatelle, fettuccine or tagliarini, first cut the sheets into approximately 20 cm (8 inch) lengths. You can then run them through the pasta cutting attachment of your pasta machine: most will have a cutting attachment approximately 1 cm (1/2 inch) wide for fettuccine or tagliatelle and 5 mm (1/4 inch) wide for taglierini.

If cutting your pasta by hand, dust the pasta sheet with Italian 00 or fine plain flour and fold it in half lengthways. Dust and fold again, then once again. Using a large, sharp knife, cut into 2.5 cm (1 inch) widths for pappardelle, 1 cm (½ inch) widths for tagliatelle or fettuccine and slightly tricky 5 mm (¼ inch) widths for taglierini.

Instructions for cutting pasta for filled pasta shapes are included in the relevant recipes.

equipment

There are only a few items that are either essential or very useful when cooking pasta or making homemade pasta and gnocchi.

large saucepan

You cannot cook pasta properly in a small saucepan! You'll need a large enough saucepan so that the pasta has plenty of space to move around in the boiling water while cooking.

colander

Once it's al dente, you'll want to drain your pasta very quickly. A large colander that you can sit in your sink is much more efficient than a sieve for this purpose.

skimmer and slotted spoon

These are great for scooping delicate filled pasta or gnocchi from the pan, rather than draining them. They are also great for serving short pasta shapes.

tongs

These make it easy to toss long pasta such as spaghetti or linguine into their sauces. They're also great for picking up the pasta when serving. Be gentle when using tongs with fresh or homemade pasta, otherwise the delicate pasta could tear.

crinkle cutter

This is used for cutting pasta sheets into lasagne sheets and/or ravioli shapes. This gadget is not essential, but it makes the job easy and adds an attractive zigzag pattern to the pasta.

mouli or ricer

This piece of equipment is essential for achieving the light, fluffy, lump-free mash needed for gnocchi. Even if you don't make gnocchi very often, these cheap tools can be used for any recipe where ingredients need to be mashed.

pasta machine

These are inexpensive and make light work of the otherwise tough job of rolling out the pasta dough by hand with a rolling pin. The attachments that cut the pasta sheets into fettuccine, tagliatelle or taglierini are also great time-savers.

ingredients

The following is a quick guide to the main ingredients used in classic Italian pasta dishes.

olive oil

There are different grades of olive oil. Extra virgin olive oil is made from the first cold pressing of olives and its rich flavour can vary from peppery to nutty or grassy. For best results, use extra virgin in recipes where the oil is not cooked or where it features as one of the main ingredients. Regular, commercially produced and less expensive olive oil is the appropriate choice in recipes where the oil is used for frying or sautéeing vegetables at the beginning of cooking.

tomatoes

There is an abundant variety of tomatoes available in Italy in summer, from juicy plum tomatoes to sweet cherry tomatoes and green salad tomatoes. Each variety has its

own use and it's the San Marzano plum tomatoes that are prized for making sauces. These are the tomatoes most commonly used for canning — either chopped or whole. Good-quality canned tomatoes should not be frowned upon and Italians happily use them in winter to make their sauces. In fact, it is far preferable to use canned tomatoes than unripened, acidic greenhouse tomatoes! Passata is smooth, raw, puréed tomatoes sold bottled or in cartons to use in cooking.

If a recipe calls for skinning tomatoes, place the tomatoes in a heatproof bowl and pour in enough boiling water to cover them. Leave for 30 seconds until the skin has loosened, then drain. Cut a small cross at the base of each tomato and pull away the skin.

cheeses

Mozzarella This can be made from cows' milk or water buffalo milk (*mozzarella di bufala*). Cows' milk mozzarella is more than adequate to use in cooking when it's going to be melted, but if you're planning to eat your mozzarella in a pasta salad, it's worth splashing out on buffalo mozzarella, as it tastes fresher and creamier. Only buy mozzarella kept in water.

Parmesan *Parmigiano Reggiano* is a cows' milk cheese made in Emilia Romana. It's extensively used grated or shaved onto pasta. *Grana Padano* is very similar to Parmesan cheese and is a more economical choice for use in cooking.

Pecorino This is sheep's milk cheese made in central and southern Italy. There are different varieties, which can be aged until they are ready for the table or matured further until dry and crumbly, to be used grated in cooking. The recipes in this book call for crumbly pecorino, often labelled *Pecorino Romano*.

Ricotta This is a naturally low-fat soft cheese made from the whey left over from cheese making. The whey is reheated, then strained into baskets to drain, hence the name *ricotta*, which means 're-cooked'. The most commonly found ricotta outside Italy is made from cows' milk and it's the one recommended for the recipes in this book.

Fontina This is a mild cheese from Piedmont, which melts evenly and smoothly, making it perfect for cooking.

Gorgonzola and dolcelatte Both these blue cheeses are frequently used in pasta sauces. Gorgonzola is the strongest, comparable to a Stilton or a Roquefort. Dolcelatte is much creamier and milder, so a better choice when making a more delicate sauce.

Mascarpone This full-fat, very thick cream cheese is mild with a rich, smooth texture.

hams

Prosciutto is the generic Italian word for ham. *Prosciutto crudo* (literally meaning 'raw ham') is the most commonly known Italian ham, of which the most famous variety is *Prosciutto di Parma* (or Parma ham). It's a raw ham cured in salt, then hung to dry and age.

Speck, a smoke-cured ham from the northern borders of Italy, is also used in this book. It has a robust, smoky flavour. Black Forest ham could be used as an alternative.

mushrooms

The most widely available wild mushrooms in Italy are porcini, chanterelles and girolles. Even during their season in autumn, Italians often use dried mushrooms, which need soaking in hot water before cooking. Of these, porcini are the most popular. Make sure that you use the soaking water from mushrooms, as it's packed with flavour!

anchovies

These small fish can be bought fresh or preserved in salt or oil. Salted anchovies taste fresher than those preserved in oil but will need thorough rinsing to remove the salt. The recipes in this book use preserved anchovy fillets rather than fresh.

capers

These are small flower buds preserved in salt or vinegar. Soak them in cold water to remove the saltiness or sharpness from the vinegar before using. Small capers are generally more flavoursome than larger buds.

flours

Italians generally use two types of soft wheat flour. They are graded as '0' flour, which is similar to regular plain flour, and '00', which is finer ground and the preferred choice for making fresh pasta. '00' flour can be bought in Italian delis and some good supermarkets. Another flour commonly used is *semola di grano duro*, a durum wheat flour used in breads and pasta. It's finer than the semolina generally used in other countries, so it's worth buying it from Italian delis, especially for making silky smooth fresh pasta.

meals for every occasion
Use these listings to help you find the appropriate pasta dish to prepare.

need for speed
Quickest-ever Tomato Pasta Sauce (page 136)
Orecchiette with Walnut Sauce (page 154)
Classic Basil Pesto (page 158)
Pesto Trapanese (page 178)
Pasta with Garlic, Oil & Chilli (page 166)

everyday supper
Pasta with Fresh Tomato & Basil (page 194)
Mascarpone & Mixed Herb Pasta (page 182)
Spaghetti & Courgette Frittata (page 210)
Spicy Tuna, Tomato & Olive Pasta (page 100)
Chicken & Tarragon Tagliatelle (page 56)

family favourites
Fettuccine all' Alfredo (page 168)
Aubergine & Rigatoni Bake (page 190)
Quick Pasta Carbonara (page 74)
Classic Bolognese (page 50)
Fettuccine with Pork Meatballs (see page 58)

warming & comforting
Autumn Minestrone (page 18)
Chunky Chickpea & Pasta Soup (page 24)
Macaroni & Haddock Cheese (page 130)
Penne with Sausage & Tomato (page 68)
Fontina, Pancetta & Sage Gnocchi (page 78)

special occasion
Wild Mushroom Pappardelle (page 146)
Farfalle with Smoked Salmon & Roe (page 122)
Rocket, Potato & Lemon Ravioli (page 220)
Duck Tortellini (page 222)
Open Seafood Lasagne (page 228)

healthy options
Broad Bean & Goats' Cheese Salad (page 30)
Spring Garden Pasta Salad (page 34)
Ricotta-baked Large Pasta Shells (page 200)
Tuna, Rocket & Lemon Conchiglie (page 88)
Linguine with Sea Bass & Tomatoes (page 104)

soups & salads

autumn minestrone

Serves **4–6**
Preparation time **15 minutes**
Cooking time **55 minutes**

2 tablespoons **olive oil**
1 **red onion**, thinly sliced
2 **carrots**, diced
2 **celery sticks**, diced
½ **fennel bulb**, trimmed and
  thinly sliced
2 **garlic cloves**, peeled
150 ml (¼ pint) **dry white
  wine**
400 g (13 oz) can **chopped
  tomatoes**
1.2 litres (2 pints) **vegetable
  stock**
1 **potato**, peeled and diced
½ x 400 g (13 oz) can
  cannellini beans, drained
  and rinsed
200 g (7 oz) **cavolo nero
  (Italian black cabbage)** or
  Savoy cabbage, shredded
75 g (3 oz) **dried small pasta
  shapes**
salt and black pepper
Classic Basil Pesto, to serve
  (optional, see page 158)

Heat the oil in a large, heavy-based saucepan over a low heat. Add the onion, carrots, celery, fennel and garlic cloves to the pan and cook, stirring occasionally, for 10 minutes. Add the wine and boil rapidly for 2 minutes. Stir in the tomatoes and stock and bring the mixture to the boil, then reduce the heat and simmer gently for 10 minutes.

Add the potato, beans and cabbage, season with salt and pepper and cook for a further 20 minutes until all the vegetables are very tender.

Add the pasta to the soup and cook, stirring frequently, until al dente. Adjust the seasoning and serve with a generous dollop of Classic Basil Pesto (see page 158), if liked.

For rich & meaty minestrone, fry 250 g (8 oz) diced gammon with the onion, carrots, celery, fennel and garlic. Replace the white wine with 300 ml (½ pint) red wine, replace the vegetable stock with the same quantity of chicken stock and use a whole can of cannellini beans.

spring minestrone

Serves **4–6**
Preparation time **15 minutes**
Cooking time **55 minutes**

2 tablespoons **olive oil**
1 **onion**, thinly sliced
2 **carrots**, diced
2 **celery sticks**, diced
2 **garlic cloves**, peeled
1 **potato**, peeled and diced
125 g (4 oz) shelled **peas**
   or **broad beans**, defrosted
   if frozen
1 **courgette**, diced
125 g (4 oz) **French beans**,
   trimmed and cut into 3.5 cm
   (1½ inch) pieces
125 g (4 oz) **plum tomatoes**,
   skinned and chopped
1.2 litres (2 pints) **vegetable
   stock**
75 g (3 oz) **dried small pasta
   shapes**
10 **basil leaves**, torn
salt and black pepper

To serve
freshly grated **Parmesan cheese**
extra virgin olive oil
toasted country bread

Heat the olive oil in a large, heavy-based saucepan over a low heat, add the onion, carrots, celery and garlic cloves and cook, stirring occasionally, for 10 minutes. Add the potato, peas or broad beans, courgette and French beans and cook, stirring frequently, for 2 minutes. Add the tomatoes, season with salt and pepper and cook for a further 2 minutes.

Pour in the stock and bring to the boil. Reduce the heat and gently simmer for 20 minutes until all the vegetables are very tender.

Add the pasta and basil to the soup and cook, stirring frequently, until the pasta is al dente. Adjust the seasoning before garnishing with a scattering of grated Parmesan and a drizzle of extra virgin olive oil. Serve with some toasted country bread.

For Parmesan toasts, to serve with the soup, toast 4–6 slices ciabatta on one side only, then brush the other side with 2–3 tablespoons olive oil and sprinkle with chilli flakes and 2 tablespoons freshly grated Parmesan. Grill under a preheated medium grill until golden and crisp.

minestrone verde

Serves **4–6**
Preparation time **20 minutes**,
   plus soaking
Cooking time **1½–1¾ hours**

50 g (2 oz) **dried cannellini
   beans**, soaked overnight
3 tablespoons **olive oil**
2 **garlic cloves**, crushed
2 **leeks**, sliced into rings
3 **tomatoes**, chopped
3 tablespoons chopped **flat
   leaf parsley**
1 tablespoon snipped **chives**,
125 g (4 oz) **French beans**, in
   2.5 cm (1 inch) lengths
150 g (5 oz) shelled **broad
   beans**, skinned
125 g (4 oz) shelled **peas**,
   fresh or frozen
1 litre (1¾ pints) **boiling water
   or stock**
75 g (3 oz) **dried small pasta
   shapes**
175 g (6 oz) **spinach**
salt and black pepper

To serve
ready-made **red pesto**
freshly grated **Parmesan**

Drain and rinse the cannellini beans, put in a saucepan and cover with cold water. Bring to the boil, then reduce the heat and simmer for 45–60 minutes until tender. Remove from the heat and set aside in their cooking water.

Heat the oil in a large saucepan over a low heat, add the garlic and leeks and cook, stirring occasionally, for 5–10 minutes until they are softened. Add the tomatoes with half the herbs, season with salt and pepper and cook for 12–15 minutes until the tomatoes have become pulpy.

Add the French beans, and the broad beans and peas, if using fresh ones. Cook for 1–2 minutes, then add the water or stock. Bring to the boil and boil rapidly for 10 minutes. Add the rice, the cooked beans and their cooking water and the spinach (and the broad beans and peas, if using frozen ones), and cook for 10 minutes. Adjust the seasoning and stir in the rest of the herbs.

Serve with a generous dollop of red pesto and a scattering of grated Parmesan, garnished with a few snipped chives.

For homemade red pepper pesto, roast 2 red peppers, then peel them and purée with 2 garlic cloves, 50 g (2 oz) pine nuts and 4 tablespoons olive oil.

chunky chickpea & pasta soup

Serves **4**
Preparation time **5 minutes**
Cooking time **35 minutes**

1 tablespoon **olive oil**
2 **garlic cloves**, finely
   chopped
2 **rosemary sprigs**, finely
   chopped
1 **dried red chilli**
2 tablespoons **tomato purée**
400 g (13 oz) can **chickpeas**,
   drained and rinsed
1.2 litres (2 pints) **vegetable**
   or **chicken stock**
175 g (6 oz) **dried tagliatelle**
   or **fettuccine**, broken into
   short lengths
salt

To serve
freshly grated **Parmesan**
   cheese
extra virgin olive oil

Heat the olive oil in a large saucepan over a low heat, add the garlic, rosemary and chilli and cook, stirring, until the garlic begins to colour. Add the tomato purée and chickpeas and cook, stirring, for 2–3 minutes, then add the stock. Bring to the boil, then reduce the heat and simmer gently for 15 minutes.

Transfer half the mixture to a food processor and process until smooth, then return to the pan. Bring to the boil and season with salt if necessary. Add the pasta and cook, stirring frequently, until al dente. Add some boiling water if the soup looks too dry, but the final dish should be thicker than the average soup, yet moister than a classic bowl of pasta.

Leave the soup to stand for 2–3 minutes before serving with a scattering of grated Parmesan and a drizzle of extra virgin olive oil.

For sausage, chickpea & pasta soup, grill 4 good-quality meaty pork sausages until brown and crisp. Slice, toss with 1 tablespoon parsley and the finely grated rind of ½ unwaxed lemon, and add to the soup when serving.

feel-good broth

Serves **4**
Preparation time **2 minutes**
Cooking time **25 minutes**

2 boneless, skinless **chicken
  breasts**, about 300 g
  (10 oz) in total
900 ml (1½ pints) **cold
  chicken stock**
1 **lemon slice**
2 teaspoons roughly chopped
  thyme
250 g (8 oz) **fresh meat
  cappelletti** or **small tortellini**
salt and black pepper
freshly grated **Parmesan
  cheese**, to serve

Put the chicken breasts, stock, lemon slice and thyme
in a large saucepan. Bring to a very gentle simmer –
the water should shiver rather than bubble in the pan.
Cover and cook for 15–16 minutes until the chicken is
opaque all the way through. Lift the chicken from the
liquid with a slotted spoon and transfer to a plate.
Remove the lemon slice.

When the chicken is cool enough to handle, shred into
large pieces.

Bring the stock to a rapid boil and season with salt
and pepper. Add the pasta and cook for 2–3 minutes,
adding the shredded chicken for the last minute of the
cooking time. Serve immediately with a generous
scattering of grated Parmesan.

For chicken broth with egg, beat two eggs well,
then remove the soup from the heat once the pasta
is cooked and gradually pour in the eggs in a steady
stream, stirring as you go. Sprinkle with 2 tablespoons
chopped tarragon and serve.

pancetta & borlotti soup

Serves **4**

Preparation time **15 minutes**, plus soaking

Cooking time **35 minutes**

15 g (½ oz) **dried porcini mushrooms**

200 ml (7 fl oz) **boiling water**

1 tablespoon **olive oil**

75 g (3 oz) **pancetta**, cut into cubes

1 small **onion**, finely chopped

1 **carrot**, finely chopped

1 **celery stick**, finely chopped

2 **garlic cloves**, finely chopped

2 **rosemary sprigs**, chopped

400 g (13 oz) can **borlotti beans**, drained and rinsed

200 ml (7 fl oz) **red wine**

1 tablespoon **tomato purée**

1 litre (1¾ pints) **chicken stock**

175 g (6 oz) **dried small pasta shapes**

salt and black pepper

To serve

freshly grated **Parmesan cheese**

extra virgin olive oil

Put the porcini in a small heatproof bowl with the measurement water, ensuring that the mushrooms are submerged. Leave to soak for 15 minutes. Drain, reserving the soaking water, and squeeze out any excess water.

Heat the olive oil in a large, heavy-based saucepan over a low heat, add the pancetta, onion, carrot and celery and cook, stirring occasionally, for 10 minutes. Increase the heat to medium-high and add the garlic, rosemary and porcini. Cook, stirring, for 1 minute, then add the beans and wine. Boil rapidly until most of the wine has evaporated. Stir in the tomato purée, reserved mushroom soaking water and stock. Bring to the boil, then reduce the heat and simmer gently for 10 minutes. The soup can be prepared ahead to this stage.

Just before serving, bring the soup to a rapid boil and season with salt and pepper. Add the pasta and cook, stirring frequently, until al dente.

Leave the soup to stand for 2–3 minutes before serving with a scattering of Parmesan and a drizzle of extra virgin olive oil.

For chunky ciabatta croûtons, to serve with the soup, chop 4 thick slices ciabatta into large cubes, toss with 2 tablespoons olive oil and 2 crushed garlic cloves and bake in a preheated oven, 180°C, 350°F, Gas Mark 4, for 10 minutes. Remove from the oven, scatter 2 teaspoons finely chopped rosemary over the cubes and return to the oven for 10 minutes or until crisp and brown. Serve hot.

broad bean & goats' cheese salad

Serves **4**
Preparation time **5 minutes**
Cooking time **15–20 minutes**

250 g (8 oz) **ripe tomatoes**
2 **garlic cloves**, peeled
5 tablespoons **extra virgin olive oil**
1 tablespoon **good-quality aged balsamic vinegar**
300 g (10 oz) shelled **broad beans**, fresh or frozen
300 g (10 oz) **dried farfalle**
200 g (7 oz) **goats' cheese**, crumbled
20 **basil leaves**, torn
salt and black pepper

Put the tomatoes and garlic in a food processor and process until the tomatoes are finely chopped. Tip into a large bowl and stir in the oil and vinegar. Season with salt and pepper.

Cook the broad beans in a saucepan of boiling water until tender: 6–8 minutes for fresh broad beans or 2 minutes if you are using frozen ones. Drain, refresh in cold water and drain again. Peel off the skins. Stir the beans into the tomato mixture and leave them to marinate while you cook the pasta.

Cook the pasta in a large saucepan of salted boiling water according to the packet instructions until al dente. Drain, refresh in cold water and then drain again. Stir the pasta into the tomato and broad bean mixture. Add the goats' cheese and basil, then toss gently. Adjust the seasoning. Leave to stand for at least 5 minutes before serving.

For fresh soya bean & pecorino farfalle salad, prepare the tomato and garlic mixture as above but replace the broad beans with 250 g (8 oz) frozen fresh soya beans, cooked for 3 minutes. Replace the goats' cheese with 60 g (2¼ oz) shaved pecorino and use 3 tablespoons finely chopped mint or flat leaf parsley instead of the basil.

warm ravioli salad with beetroot

Serves **4**
Preparation time **10 minutes**
Cooking time **12 minutes**

4 tablespoons **extra virgin olive oil**
2 **red onions**, thinly sliced
2 **garlic cloves**, thinly sliced
500 g (1 lb) **fresh spinach and ricotta ravioli**
375 g (12 oz) **cooked beetroot** in natural juices, drained and diced
2 tablespoons **capers** in brine, rinsed and drained
2 tablespoons **good-quality aged balsamic vinegar**
salt

To serve
mixed bitter salad leaves, such as chicory, radicchio, rocket and frisée
parsley sprigs
basil leaves
fresh **pecorino cheese shavings** (optional)

Heat 2 tablespoons of the oil in a large frying pan over a medium heat, add the onions and garlic and cook, stirring occasionally, for 10 minutes until golden.

Meanwhile, cook the pasta in a large saucepan of salted boiling water according to the packet instructions until al dente. Drain and gently toss with the remaining oil.

Add the beetroot, capers and vinegar to the onions and garlic in the pan and heat through. Stir into the pasta. Transfer to a large bowl, including all the juices from the pan, and leave to cool for 5 minutes.

Arrange the ravioli in serving bowls or on plates with the salad leaves and herbs. Serve with a scattering of pecorino shavings, if you like.

For penne salad with beetroot & ricotta, replace the ravioli with 200 g (7 oz) penne. Cook the pasta and combine with the sauce, as above, then finish with 100 g (3½ oz) crumbled ricotta cheese.

spring garden pasta salad

Serves **4**
Preparation time **10 minutes**
Cooking time **10–12 minutes**

4 tablespoons **extra virgin
    olive oil**
1 **garlic clove**, crushed
finely grated **rind and juice
    of** ½ **unwaxed lemon**
6 **spring onions**, thinly sliced
175 g (6 oz) **dried fusilli**
150 g (5 oz) **asparagus tips**,
    cut into 2.5 cm (1 inch)
    pieces
150 g (5 oz) **green beans**,
    trimmed and cut into 2.5 cm
    (1 inch) pieces
50g (2 oz) shelled **peas**, fresh
    or frozen
1 **buffalo mozzarella cheese
    ball**, drained and torn into
    small pieces
50 g (2 oz) **watercress**
2 tablespoons roughly
    chopped **flat leaf parsley**
2 tablespoons snipped **chives**
8 **basil leaves**, torn
salt and black pepper

Mix the oil, garlic, lemon rind and juice and spring onions together in a large, non-metallic serving bowl and leave to infuse while you cook the pasta.

Cook the pasta in a large saucepan of salted boiling water according to the packet instructions until al dente, adding the asparagus, beans and peas to the pan 3 minutes before the end of the cooking time.

Drain the pasta and vegetables lightly, then stir into the prepared dressing. Set aside in a cool place until cooled to room temperature.

Fold the remaining ingredients into the pasta salad. Season with salt and pepper, then leave the dish to stand for at least 5 minutes for the flavours to mingle before serving.

For sugar snap pea & broad bean salad, replace the asparagus tips with 150 g (5 oz) sugar snap peas and the green beans with 150 g (5 oz) broad beans. Cut the sugar snaps in half and add them, together with the beans, to the pan 3–5 minutes before the end of the pasta cooking time. Replace the watercress with 50 g (2 oz) rocket.

aubergine & courgette pasta salad

Serves **4**
Preparation time **10 minutes**,
  plus marinating and standing
Cooking time **25 minutes**

1 **aubergine**, cut into 1 cm
  (½ inch) slices
2 **courgettes**, cut into 1 cm
  (½ inch) slices
100 ml (3½ fl oz) **extra virgin
  olive oil**
1 tablespoon **good-quality
  aged balsamic vinegar**
3 **garlic cloves**, finely
  chopped
20 g (¾ oz) **basil**, roughly
  chopped
20 g (¾ oz) **mint**, roughly
  chopped
2 tablespoons **capers** in brine,
  rinsed and drained
1 **fresh red chilli**, deseeded
  and finely chopped
40 g (1½ oz) **pine nuts**
200 g (7 oz) **dried conchiglie**
salt

Heat a ridged griddle pan over a high heat until
smoking. Toss the aubergines and courgettes with
4 tablespoons of the oil in a bowl. Add to the pan,
in batches, and cook for 1–2 minutes on each side
until well charred and tender all the way through.

As you remove the batches from the pan, cut the
courgette slices into 3 and the aubergine slices in
half. Transfer the vegetables to a bowl with the
remaining oil, vinegar, garlic, herbs, capers and chilli,
and toss well to combine. Season with salt and leave
to marinate for at least 20 minutes, or up to overnight,
covered, in the refrigerator.

Toast the pine nuts in a dry frying pan over a low heat,
stirring frequently, for 2–3 minutes, or until golden. Stir
into the griddled vegetables.

Cook the pasta in a large saucepan of salted boiling
water according to the packet instructions until al
dente. Drain, refresh in cold water, then drain again
thoroughly before stirring into the prepared griddled
vegetables. Leave to stand for 10 minutes for the
flavours to mingle before serving.

For red pepper & asparagus salad, replace the
aubergine and courgettes with 2 red peppers and
150 g (5 oz) asparagus. Halve, deseed and slice the
red peppers and trim, blanch and drain the asparagus.
Griddle the peppers and asparagus and prepare the
rest of the salad as above.

artichoke, pea & mint salad

Serves **4**

Preparation time **10 minutes**, plus standing

Cooking time **10 minutes**

250 g (8 oz) **dried small pasta shapes**

250 g (8 oz) **frozen peas**, defrosted

5 tablespoons **extra virgin olive oil**

6 **spring onions**, roughly chopped

2 **garlic cloves**, crushed

8 **bottled marinated artichoke hearts**, drained and thickly sliced

4 tablespoons chopped **mint**

finely grated **rind and juice of** ½ **unwaxed lemon**, plus extra grated rind to garnish

salt and black pepper

Cook the pasta in a large saucepan of salted boiling water according to the packet instructions until al dente, adding the peas to the pan 3 minutes before the end of the cooking time. Drain thoroughly.

Meanwhile, heat 2 tablespoons of the oil in a frying pan over a medium heat, add the spring onions and garlic and cook, stirring, for 1–2 minutes until softened.

Stir in the pasta and peas with the artichokes, mint and remaining oil. Toss well, season with salt and pepper, then leave to stand for 10 minutes. Stir in the lemon rind and juice and serve the salad warm, garnished with lemon rind.

For prosciutto, asparagus, pea & mint salad,
replace the artichoke with 250 g (8 oz) asparagus spears and 150 g (5 oz) prosciutto. Trim any thick ends from the asparagus and steam for 3–5 minutes (depending on thickness). Grill the prosciutto until crisp. Prepare the rest of the salad as described above, serving with the asparagus on top and the prosciutto crumbled over.

herby bean & feta salad

Serves **2**
Preparation time **15 minutes**
Cooking time **10–12 minutes**

200 g (7 oz) **dried penne** or
other **pasta shapes**
200 g (7 oz) shelled **broad
beans**, fresh or frozen
50 g (2 oz) **sun-blush
(semi-dried) tomatoes** in
oil, drained and roughly
chopped
handful of **mixed herbs**, such
as parsley, tarragon, chervil
and chives, roughly chopped
50 g (2 oz) **feta cheese**,
crumbled or roughly
chopped
salt and black pepper

Dressing
2 tablespoons **extra virgin
olive oil**
1 tablespoon **sherry vinegar**
½ teaspoon **wholegrain
mustard**

Cook the pasta in a large saucepan of salted boiling water according to the packet instructions until al dente. Drain, refresh in cold water and drain thoroughly.

Meanwhile, cook the broad beans in a separate saucepan of lightly salted boiling water for 4–5 minutes until just tender. Drain and plunge into ice-cold water to cool. Peel off the skins.

Whisk the dressing ingredients together in a small bowl and season with salt and pepper.

Put the beans in a serving dish and stir in the pasta, tomatoes and herbs. Toss with the dressing. Season with pepper and scatter over the feta. Serve immediately.

For bean & two cheeses pasta salad, use a 150 g (5 oz) buffalo mozzarella ball and 50 g (2 oz) Gorgonzola. Dice the cheeses and sprinkle on top of the salad instead of the feta.

meat &
poultry

chorizo carbonara

Serves **4**
Preparation time **5 minutes**
Cooking time **18–20 minutes**

125 g (4 oz) **chorizo
   sausage**, sliced
1 tablespoon **olive oil**
375 g (12 oz) **dried penne**
4 **eggs**
50 g (2 oz) **Parmesan
   cheese**, freshly grated,
   plus extra to serve
salt and black pepper

Put the chorizo and oil in a frying pan over a very low heat and cook, turning occasionally, until crisp. The melted fat released by the chorizo will be an essential part of your sauce.

Cook the pasta in a large saucepan of salted boiling water according to the packet instructions until it is al dente.

Meanwhile, crack the eggs into a bowl, add the Parmesan and season with salt and a generous grinding of pepper. Mix together with a fork.

Just before the pasta is ready, increase the heat under the frying pan so that the oil and melted chorizo fat start to sizzle. Drain the pasta thoroughly, return to the pan and immediately stir in the egg mixture and the sizzling-hot contents of the frying pan. Stir vigorously so that the eggs cook evenly. Serve immediately with a scattering of grated Parmesan.

For spicy chorizo & leek carbonara, fry 1 finely sliced leek in 2 tablespoons olive oil for 6–8 minutes until soft, then add the chorizo and cook as above. Add ½ teaspoon hot paprika to the egg mixture and complete the recipe as above.

speck, spinach & taleggio fusilli

Serves **4**
Preparation time **5 minutes**
Cooking time **15 minutes**

375 g (12 oz) **dried fusilli**
100 g (3½ oz) **speck slices**
150 g (5 oz) **Taleggio
    cheese**, cut into small cubes
150 ml (½ pint) **double cream**
125 g (4 oz) **baby spinach**,
    roughly chopped
salt and black pepper
freshly grated **Parmesan
    cheese**, to serve (optional)

Cook the pasta in a large saucepan of salted boiling water according to the packet instructions until it is al dente.

Meanwhile, cut the speck into wide strips.

Drain the pasta, return to the pan and place over a low heat. Add the speck, Taleggio, cream and spinach and stir until most of the cheese has melted. Season with a generous grinding of pepper and serve immediately with a scattering of grated Parmesan, if liked.

For mozzarella & ham fusilli, use 150 g (5 oz) mozzarella instead of the Taleggio and replace the speck with 100 g (3½ oz) Black Forest ham. Mozzarella will give a milder flavour than Taleggio.

pasta arrabiata with garlic crumbs

Serves **4–6**
Preparation time **5 minutes**
Cooking time **30 minutes**

3 tablespoons **olive oil**
2 **shallots**, finely chopped
8 slices of **unsmoked pancetta**, chopped
2 teaspoons **crushed dried chillies**
500 g (1 lb) **canned chopped tomatoes**
400–600 g (13 oz–1 lb 2 oz) **dried pasta** of your choice
salt and black pepper
parsley sprigs, to garnish

Mollica
4 slices of **white bread**, crusts removed
125 g (4 oz) **butter**
2 **garlic cloves**, finely chopped

Heat the oil in a saucepan over a medium heat, add the shallots and pancetta and cook, stirring frequently, for 6–8 minutes until golden. Add the chillies and tomatoes, partially cover the pan and simmer for 20 minutes until the sauce is thick and has reduced. Season with salt and pepper.

Meanwhile, cook the pasta in a large saucepan of salted boiling water according to the packet instructions until al dente.

To make the mollica, put the bread in a food processor and process to crumbs. Melt the butter in a frying pan over a medium-high heat, add the breadcrumbs and garlic and cook, stirring, until golden and crisp. (Don't let the crumbs burn, or the dish will be ruined!)

Drain the pasta and toss with the tomato sauce. Serve immediately with a scattering of the garlic crumbs, garnished with parsley sprigs.

For pepper arrabiata, grill 3 halved red peppers for 10 minutes or until their skins are blackened. Remove the charred skins and chop the flesh, add to 250 g (8 oz) chopped tomatoes and proceed as above.

classic bolognese

Serves **4**
Preparation time **10 minutes**
Cooking time **4–6 hours**

25 g (1 oz) **unsalted butter**
1 tablespoon **olive oil**
1 small **onion**, finely chopped
2 **celery sticks**, finely chopped
1 **carrot**, finely chopped
1 **bay leaf**
200 g (7 oz) **lean minced beef**
200 g (7 oz) **lean minced pork**
150 ml (¼ pint) **dry white wine**
150 ml (¼ pint) **milk**
large pinch of freshly grated **nutmeg**
2 x 400 g (13 oz) cans **chopped tomatoes**
400–600 ml (14 fl oz–1 pint) **chicken stock**
400 g (13 oz) **dried fettuccine** or **homemade fettuccine** using 1 quantity 3-egg Pasta Dough (see page 10)
salt and black pepper
freshly grated **Parmesan cheese**, to serve

Melt the butter with the oil in a large, heavy-based saucepan over a low heat. Add the onion, celery, carrot and bay leaf and cook, stirring occasionally, for 10 minutes until softened but not coloured. Add the meat, season with salt and pepper and cook, stirring, over a medium heat until no longer pink.

Pour in the wine and bring to the boil. Gently simmer for 15 minutes until evaporated. Stir in the milk and nutmeg and simmer for a further 15 minutes until the milk has evaporated. Stir in the tomatoes and cook, uncovered, over a very low heat for 3–5 hours. The sauce is very thick, so when it begins to stick, add 100 ml (3½ fl oz) of the stock at a time, as needed.

Cook the pasta in a large saucepan of salted boiling water until al dente: according to the packet instructions for dried pasta or for 2 minutes if you are using fresh pasta. Drain thoroughly, reserving a ladleful of the cooking water.

Return to the pan and place over a low heat. Add the sauce and stir for 30 seconds, then pour in the reserved pasta cooking water and stir until the pasta is well coated and looks silky. Serve immediately with a scattering of grated Parmesan.

For rich pork & chicken liver bolognaise, dice 100 g (3½ oz) chicken liver and 100 g (3½ oz) pancetta and cook with the onion in step 1. Replace the beef with 200 g (7 oz) minced pork and proceed as above.

broccoli & sausage orecchiette

Serves **4**
Preparation time **5 minutes**
Cooking time **15 minutes**

2 tablespoons **olive oil**
1 **onion**, finely chopped
200 g (7 oz) **Italian pork sausage**
large pinch of **crushed dried chillies**
300 g (10 oz) **dried orecchiette**
200 g (7 oz) **broccoli**, broken into florets
40 g (1¼ oz) **pecorino cheese**, freshly grated, plus extra to serve
salt

Heat the oil in a frying pan over a low heat, add the onion and cook, stirring occasionally, for 6–7 minutes until softened. Split the sausage open and break up the sausagemeat with a fork. Add the sausagemeat chunks and chillies to the pan and increase the heat to medium. Cook, stirring, for 4–5 minutes until the sausagemeat is golden brown.

Meanwhile, cook the pasta and broccoli in a large saucepan of salted boiling water according to the pasta packet instructions until the pasta is al dente. Don't be alarmed if the broccoli starts to break up – it needs to be very tender.

Drain the pasta and broccoli and toss into the frying pan with the sausagemeat. Stir in the pecorino and serve immediately with a bowl of extra grated pecorino on the side.

For cauliflower & chorizo sauce, replace the Italian pork sausage with 200 g (7 oz) sliced chorizo. Cut 250 g (8 oz) cauliflower into small florets and cook with the pasta as above.

pancetta, tomato & onion bucatini

Serves **4**
Preparation time **5 minutes**
Cooking time **1 hour**

1 tablespoon **olive oil**
1 **onion**, finely chopped
125 g (4 oz) **pancetta**, cut
    into cubes
2 **garlic cloves**, crushed
1 **dried red chilli**, finely
    chopped
2 x 400 g (13 oz) cans
    chopped tomatoes
400 g (13 oz) **dried bucatini**
freshly grated **Parmesan** or
    pecorino cheese, to serve
    (optional)
salt and pepper

Put the oil, onion and pancetta in a frying pan over a low heat and cook, stirring occasionally, for 7–8 minutes until the onion is soft and the pancetta is golden. Add the garlic and chilli and cook, stirring, for 1 minute, then stir in the tomatoes. Season with salt and pepper and bring to the boil. Reduce the heat and simmer very gently for 40 minutes, adding a little water if the sauce begins to stick. The sauce can be prepared ahead up to this stage, if you like.

Cook the pasta in a large saucepan of salted boiling water according to the packet instructions until al dente. Drain, reserving a ladleful of the cooking water. Return the pasta to the saucepan.

If the sauce was prepared ahead, heat through before adding it to the pasta. Stir over a medium heat to combine, then add the reserved pasta cooking water and continue stirring until the pasta is well coated and looks silky. Serve immediately with a scattering of grated Parmesan or pecorino, if liked.

For mushroom & walnut bucatini, replace the pancetta with an extra onion and 350 g (11½ oz) mushrooms. Dice the mushrooms and fry them with the onions until they are thoroughly reduced. Prepare the rest of the sauce as above and serve sprinkled with the Parmesan or pecorino and 50 g (2 oz) chopped walnuts.

chicken & tarragon tagliatelle

Serves **4**

Preparation time **15 minutes**, plus marinating

Cooking time **10–15 minutes**

3 boneless, skinless **chicken breasts**, about 450 g (14½ oz) in total, cut into thin strips

1 **garlic clove**, finely chopped

finely grated **rind and juice of 1 unwaxed lemon**

1 tablespoon **olive oil**

125 g (4 oz) **frozen broad beans**, defrosted and skinned

250 ml (8 fl oz) **crème fraîche**

2 tablespoons roughly chopped **tarragon**

400 g (13 oz) **dried tagliatelle** or **homemade tagliatelle** using 1 quantity 3-egg Pasta Dough (see page 10)

salt and black pepper

Put the chicken strips with the garlic and half the lemon rind and juice in a non-metallic bowl and turn to coat in the marinade. Cover and leave to marinate in a cool place for 15 minutes.

Heat the oil in a large frying pan over a high heat. Season the chicken with salt and pepper, add to the pan and cook, stirring, for 2 minutes. Add the broad beans and cook, stirring, for a further minute until the chicken is golden and cooked through. Stir in the crème fraîche, tarragon and remaining lemon rind and juice. Season with salt and pepper and remove from the heat immediately the sauce reaches boiling point.

Cook the pasta in a large saucepan of salted boiling water until al dente: according to packet instructions for dried pasta or for 2 minutes if you are using fresh pasta. Drain thoroughly, reserving a ladleful of the cooking water.

Tip the pasta into the sauce and toss over a low heat until well combined. If the sauce looks too dry, add a little of the reserved pasta cooking water to give it a silky consistency.

For salmon & tarragon tagliatelle, dice 400 g (13 oz) skinless boneless salmon fillets and use in place of the chicken. Replace the broad beans with fine green beans cut into short lengths and use 2 tablespoons chopped dill instead of the tarragon.

fettuccine with pork meatballs

Serves **6**

Preparation time **20 minutes**,
  plus chilling

Cooking time **45 minutes**

400 g (13 oz) **dried
  fettuccine or tagliatelle**

1 slice of **white bread**, crust
  removed, broken into small
  pieces

3 tablespoons **milk**

300 g (10 oz) **minced pork**

1 **egg**

½ **onion**, very finely chopped

2 tablespoons chopped **flat
  leaf parsley**

½ teaspoon **salt**

4 tablespoons **olive oil**

1 **garlic clove**, crushed

2 x 400 g (13 oz) cans
  chopped tomatoes

100 g (3½ oz) **bottled,
  drained roasted peppers**,
  cut into strips

1 tablespoon **dried oregano**

large pinch of **caster sugar**

salt and black pepper

extra virgin olive oil, to serve

For the meatballs, soak the bread in milk for 5 minutes. Squeeze out and crumble between your fingers into a bowl. Add the pork, egg, onion and parsley. Stir in the salt and when well combined shape into small meatballs. Cover and chill for at least 20 minutes.

Meanwhile, for the sauce, heat half the olive oil in a wide saucepan over a low heat. Add the garlic and cook, stirring, for 1 minute. Add the tomatoes, peppers, oregano and sugar and bring to the boil. Reduce the heat and season with salt and pepper. Cover and simmer gently for 10 minutes.

Heat the remaining olive oil in a frying pan over a high heat, add the meatballs, in batches, and cook until golden brown. Add to the sauce. Pour a cup of water into the frying pan and bring to a rapid boil, scraping up any sediment from the base. Pour into the sauce and simmer, covered, for a further 20 minutes.

When the sauce is almost ready, cook the pasta in a large saucepan of salted boiling water according to the packet instructions until al dente. Drain thoroughly and toss into the sauce. Serve with a drizzle of extra virgin olive oil.

For classic mixed green salad, to serve with the fettuccine, deseed and slice 1 green pepper, shred 2 Little Gem lettuce hearts, finely chop 4 spring onions, slice ½ cucumber and mix with 50 g (2 oz) watercress. Drizzle with a little olive oil and balsamic vinegar before serving.

asparagus & bacon farfalle

Serves **4**
Preparation time **10 minutes**
Cooking time **15 minutes**

400 g (13 oz) **asparagus**, trimmed
1 large **garlic clove**, crushed
4 tablespoons **olive oil**
50 g (2 oz) **Parmesan cheese**, freshly grated
8 **streaky bacon** or **pancetta rashers**
400 g (13 oz) **dried farfalle**
salt and black pepper
fresh **Parmesan cheese shavings**, to serve

Cut the tips off the asparagus and reserve. Cut the stalks into 2.5 cm (1 inch) pieces and blanch in a saucepan of boiling water for 3–4 minutes until very tender. Drain and put in a food processor with the garlic, oil and Parmesan. Process to make a smooth paste. Season with salt and pepper.

Arrange the bacon rashers in a single layer on a baking sheet and cook under a preheated hot grill for 5–6 minutes until crisp and golden. Break into 2.5 cm (1 inch) lengths.

Meanwhile, cook the pasta in a large saucepan of salted boiling water according to the packet instructions until al dente, adding the reserved asparagus tips to the pan 3 minutes before the end of the cooking time.

Drain the pasta and stir into a bowl with the asparagus sauce. Scatter with the crispy bacon and Parmesan shavings and serve immediately.

For creamy courgette & bacon farfalle, omit the asparagus tips and instead pan-fry 250 g (8 oz) sliced small courgettes in 25 g (1 oz) butter while the pasta is cooking and the bacon grilling. When cooked, toss the pasta with the courgette and the bacon and 4 tablespoons single cream.

radicchio, speck & onion fusilli

Serves **4**
Preparation time **10 minutes**
Cooking time **25 minutes**

5 tablespoons **extra virgin olive oil**, plus extra to serve
1 **onion**, thinly sliced
125 g (4 oz) **speck slices**, cut into strips
1 **garlic clove**, thinly sliced
200 g (7 oz) **radicchio**, shredded
400 g (13 oz) **dried fusilli**
salt and black pepper

Heat the oil in a large frying pan over a low heat, add the onion and cook, stirring occasionally, for 6–7 minutes until softened. Increase the heat to high and add the speck, garlic and radicchio. Cook, stirring, for 4–5 minutes until the radicchio is wilted and tender. Season with salt and pepper.

Cook the pasta in a large saucepan of salted boiling water according to the packet instructions until al dente. Drain, reserving a ladleful of the cooking water.

Return the frying pan with the radicchio mixture to a low heat and toss in the pasta. Combine well, then add the reserved pasta cooking water and continue stirring until the pasta is well coated and looks silky. Serve immediately with a drizzle of oil.

For spring greens & gammon with pasta, replace the speck with 125 g (4 oz) finely diced gammon and replace the radicchio with 200 g (7 oz) shredded spring greens. Cook as above, drizzling the sauce with 2 tablespoons balsamic vinegar before serving.

roast meat ragù

Serves **4**
Preparation time **15 minutes**
Cooking time **45–55 minutes**

25 g (1 oz) **unsalted butter**
1 tablespoon **olive oil**
1 small **onion**, finely chopped
1 **celery stick**, finely chopped
1 **carrot**, finely chopped
2 tablespoons chopped **thyme**
pinch **crushed dried chillies**
2 **garlic cloves**, crushed
300 g (10 oz) **roasted beef,
    lamb, pork or poultry,**
    shredded or cut into strips
200 ml (7 fl oz) **dry white wine**
400 g (13 oz) can **tomatoes**
200 ml (7 fl oz) **meat stock**
2 tablespoons roughly
    chopped **flat leaf parsley**
finely grated **rind of 1
    unwaxed lemon**
2 tablespoons **extra virgin
    olive oil**, plus extra if needed
400 g (13 oz) **dried
    pappardelle** or homemade
    pappardelle using 1
    quantity 3-egg Pasta Dough
    (see page 10)
salt
freshly grated **Parmesan
    cheese**, to serve (optional)

Melt the butter with the olive oil in a large heavy-based saucepan over a low heat. Add the onion, celery and carrot and cook for 10 minutes, stirring occasionally, until softened but not coloured. Increase the heat to high, add the thyme, chillies, garlic and meat and cook, stirring, for 30 seconds. Pour in the wine and boil rapidly for 2 minutes, then add the tomatoes and stock and season with salt.

Bring to the boil, then reduce the heat and simmer gently, uncovered, for 30–35 minutes until thickened. Remove from the heat, stir in the parsley, lemon rind and extra virgin olive oil and cover while you cook the pasta.

Cook the pasta in a large saucepan of salted boiling water until al dente: according to the packet instructions for dried pasta or 2 minutes if using fresh pasta. Drain and return to the pan. Toss in the meat sauce, adding more extra virgin olive oil, if needed. Serve immediately with a scattering of grated Parmesan, if liked.

For simple courgette salad, to serve as a refreshing side dish, coarsely grate 4 firm young courgettes and combine with 6 finely shredded basil leaves, 1 chopped spring onion and a drizzle of olive oil. Serve the salad with lemon wedges.

peas, speck & mint rigatoni

Serves **4**
Preparation time **10 minutes**
Cooking time **15 minutes**

25 g (1 oz) **unsalted butter**
2 tablespoons **olive oil**
2 **shallots**, cut into thin
  wedges
100 g (3½ oz) **speck slices**,
  cut into strips
200 ml (7 fl oz) **dry white
  wine**
400 g (13 oz) shelled **peas**,
  defrosted if frozen
2 tablespoons roughly
  chopped **mint**, plus extra
  leaves to garnish
400 g (13 oz) **dried rigatoni**
salt and black pepper
fresh **Parmesan cheese
  shavings**, to serve

Melt the butter with the oil in a frying pan over a
medium heat, add the shallots and cook, stirring
occasionally, for 5 minutes. Add the speck strips and
cook, stirring frequently, for 2–3 minutes until crisp.
Pour in the wine and simmer for 2 minutes until the
mixture is slightly reduced.

Add the peas and mint and cook, stirring occasionally,
for 5 minutes if using fresh peas, or 2 minutes if using
defrosted frozen peas. Season with salt and pepper.

Meanwhile, cook the pasta in a large saucepan
of salted boiling water according to the packet
instructions until al dente. Drain quickly, then toss into
the frying pan with the pea mixture. Serve immediately
with a scattering of Parmesan shavings, garnished with
mint leaves.

For pancetta, mint & Brussels sprouts pasta,
replace the speck with 100 g (3½ oz) diced pancetta.
Slice 200 g (7 oz) Brussels sprouts and cook with
the pancetta for 2 minutes before adding the wine
and continuing as above.

penne with sausage & tomato

Serves **4**

Preparation time **5 minutes**

Cooking time **45 minutes**

2 tablespoons **olive oil**

1 large **onion**, finely chopped

250 g (8 oz) **Italian pork sausage**

½ teaspoon **fennel seeds**

1 **dried red chilli**, finely chopped

1 **celery stick**, kept whole

1 **bay leaf**

200 ml (7 fl oz) **red wine**

625 g (1¼ lb) **canned chopped tomatoes**

4 tablespoons **milk**

400 g (13 oz) **dried penne** or **rigatoni**

salt

freshly grated **Parmesan** or **pecorino cheese**, to serve

Heat the oil in a frying pan over a low heat, add the onion and cook, stirring occasionally, for 6–7 minutes until softened. Split the sausage open and break up the sausagemeat with a fork. Add the sausagemeat chunks, fennel seeds and chilli to the pan and increase the heat to medium. Cook, stirring, for 4–5 minutes, until the sausagemeat is golden brown.

Add the celery, bay leaf and wine and simmer until most of the wine has evaporated. Stir in the tomatoes, season with salt and bring to the boil. Reduce the heat and simmer for 25–30 minutes until thick. Stir in the milk and simmer for a further 5 minutes. Remove the celery stick and bay leaf from the sauce.

Meanwhile, cook the pasta in a large saucepan of salted boiling water according to the packet instructions until al dente.

Drain the pasta and stir into the sauce. Serve immediately with some grated Parmesan or pecorino on the side.

For aubergine, sausage & olive penne, trim, slice and dice 1 aubergine, add to the pan with the sausagemeat and cook as above. Sprinkle the sauce with 25 g (1 oz) chopped black olives before serving.

chestnut & sausage tagliatelle

Serves **4**
Preparation time **10 minutes**
Cooking time **10–20 minutes**

200 g (7 oz) **Italian pork sausage**
75 g (3 oz) **canned or vacuum-packed chestnuts**, drained and roughly chopped
2 tablespoons roughly chopped **thyme**
200 ml (7 fl oz) **double cream**
400 g (13 oz) **dried tagliatelle or homemade tagliatelle** using 1 quantity 3-egg Pasta Dough (see page 10)
50 g (2 oz) **Parmesan cheese**, freshly grated, plus extra to serve (optional)
5 tablespoons **milk**
salt and black pepper
fresh **thyme sprig**, to serve

Split the sausage open and break up the sausagemeat with a fork. Heat a large, heavy-based frying pan over a low heat, add the sausagemeat chunks and cook, stirring, until they are lightly golden. As the fat from the sausages heats, it will melt and stop the meat from sticking to the pan.

Increase the heat to high and stir in the chestnuts and thyme. Cook, stirring, for 1–2 minutes to colour the chestnuts, then pour in the cream and simmer gently for 1 minute until slightly thickened.

Cook the pasta in a large saucepan of salted boiling water until it is al dente: according to the packet instructions for dried pasta or for 2 minutes if using fresh pasta. Drain thoroughly, then toss into the sauce.

Place over a very low heat and add the Parmesan and milk. Season with salt and pepper. Toss gently until the sauce has thickened and the pasta is well coated with the sauce. Serve immediately with a scattering of grated Parmesan, if liked.

For spicy sausagemeat, to use in the recipe in place of Italian pork sausage, combine a pinch of dried chilli flakes, 2 crushed garlic cloves, 1 tablespoon ground coriander and 1 tablespoon ground fennel seeds with ordinary pork sausagemeat. Mix well, separate into lumps and cook as above.

classic meat lasagne

Serves **6–8**

Preparation time **20 minutes**, plus infusing

Cooking time **27–35 minutes**

750 ml (1¼ pints) **milk**
1 **bay leaf**
50 g (2 oz) **unsalted butter**
50 g (2 oz) **plain flour**
large pinch of freshly grated **nutmeg**
1 quantity **Classic Bolognese sauce** (see page 50)
250 g (8 oz) **dried lasagne sheets** or **1 quantity 2-egg Pasta Dough** (see page 10), rolled out to lasagne sheets
5 tablespoons freshly grated **Parmesan cheese**
salt and black pepper

Make the béchamel sauce. Bring the milk and bay leaf to a simmer. Infuse off the heat for 20 minutes. Strain. Melt the butter in a separate pan over a very low heat. Add the flour and cook, stirring, for 2 minutes until a light biscuity colour. Remove from the heat and slowly add the infused milk, stirring away lumps. Return to the heat and simmer, stirring, for 2–3 minutes until creamy. Add the nutmeg and season with salt and pepper.

If your Bolognese sauce was made earlier, reheat in a small pan or a microwave oven. Meanwhile, cook the pasta sheets, in batches, in salted boiling water until just al dente: according to packet instructions for dried pasta or for 2 minutes if using fresh pasta. Drain, refresh in cold water and lay on a tea towel to drain.

Cover the base of an ovenproof dish with one-third of the Bolognese sauce, top with a layer of pasta and cover with half the remaining Bolognese, then one-third of the béchamel sauce. Repeat with a layer of pasta, the remaining Bolognese and half the remaining béchamel sauce. Finish with the remaining pasta, then spoon over the remaining béchamel and scatter with Parmesan. Bake in a preheated oven, 220°C (425°F), Gas Mark 7, for 20 minutes until golden brown.

For sausage & two-cheese lasagna, replace the Bolognese with 1 quantity Sausage & Tomato sauce (see page 68). Omit the béchamel and use 200 g (7 oz) fontina cheese, dotted over the tomato sauce. Top the lasagna with 250 g (7 oz) chopped mozzarella, pour over 4 tablespoons milk and bake as above.

quick pasta carbonara

Serves **4**

Preparation time **10 minutes**

Cooking time **10 minutes**

400 g (13 oz) **dried spaghetti**
or **other long thin pasta**

2 tablespoons **olive oil**

200 g (7 oz) **pancetta**, cut
into cubes

3 **eggs**

4 tablespoons freshly grated
Parmesan cheese

3 tablespoons chopped **flat
leaf parsley**

3 tablespoons **single cream**

salt and black pepper

Cook the pasta in a large saucepan of boiling salted water according to the packet instructions until al dente.

Meanwhile, heat the oil in a large, nonstick frying pan over a medium heat, add the pancetta and cook, stirring frequently, for 4–5 minutes until crisp.

Beat the eggs with the Parmesan, parsley and cream in a bowl. Season with salt and pepper and set aside.

Drain the pasta and add to the pancetta mixture. Stir over a low heat until combined, then pour in the egg mixture. Stir and remove the pan from the heat. Continue stirring for a few seconds until the eggs are lightly cooked and creamy. Serve immediately.

For mushroom carbonara, add 100 g (3½ oz) sliced mushrooms with the pancetta and cook as above.

mushroom & parma ham lasagne

Serves **8**

Preparation time **25 minutes**,
  plus soaking and infusing

Cooking time **35–40 minutes**

20 g (¾ oz) **dried porcini
  mushrooms**

750 ml (1¼ pints) **milk**

1 **bay leaf**

1 small **onion**, quartered

125 g (4 oz) **unsalted butter**

30 g (1¼ oz) **plain flour**

175 ml (6 fl oz) **single cream**

¼ teaspoon freshly grated
  nutmeg

200 g (7 oz) **Parma ham**,
  4 whole slices, remainder
  torn into strips

3 tablespoons **olive oil**

325 g (11 oz) **chestnut
  mushrooms**, chopped

50 ml (2 fl oz) **dry white wine**

250 g (8 oz) **dried lasagne
  sheets**

5 tablespoons freshly grated
  Parmesan cheese

salt and black pepper

Soak the porcini in a little boiling water for 30 minutes. Meanwhile, bring the milk with the bay leaf and onion to a simmer. Infuse off the heat for 20 minutes. Strain. Melt 50 g (2 oz) of the butter in a saucepan over a very low heat. Add the flour and cook, stirring, for 2 minutes until a light biscuity colour. Remove from the heat and slowly add the infused milk, stirring away any lumps as you go. Return to the heat and simmer, stirring, for 2–3 minutes until creamy. Add the cream, nutmeg and ham strips. Season with salt and pepper.

Drain the porcini, reserving the soaking water, and chop. Heat the oil in a frying pan over a high heat, add all the mushrooms and cook for 1 minute. Add the soaking water and wine. Boil rapidly until absorbed. Season and stir into the sauce.

Cook the pasta sheets, in batches, in boiling salted water according to the packet instructions until just al dente. Refresh in cold water. Drain on a tea towel.

Lightly grease an ovenproof dish. Cover the base with a layer of pasta. Top with a quarter of the sauce. Dot with a quarter of the remaining butter, then scatter with 1 tablespoon Parmesan. Repeat, finishing with a layer of sauce topped with the ham slices and remaining butter and Parmesan. Bake in a preheated oven, 220°C (425°F), Gas Mark 7, for 20 minutes until browned.

fontina, pancetta & sage gnocchi

Serves **4**
Preparation time **2 minutes**
Cooking time **20 minutes**

15 g (½ oz) **unsalted butter**
125 g (4 oz) **pancetta**, cut
   into cubes
200 ml (7 fl oz) **double cream**
6 **sage leaves**, cut into thin
   strips
75 g (3 oz) **fontina cheese**,
   cut into cubes
4 tablespoons freshly grated
   Parmesan cheese
500 g (1 lb) bought **gnocchi
   or 1 quantity Classic Potato
   Gnocchi** (see page 218)
salt and black pepper

Melt the butter in a large frying pan over a low heat,
add the pancetta and cook, stirring occasionally, for
10–12 minutes until crisp.

Stir in the cream and sage, increase the heat to high
and bring to the boil. Boil until slightly thickened. Stir in
the fontina and Parmesan, then remove from the heat.
Stir until most of the cheese has melted, then season
with salt and pepper.

Cook the gnocchi in a large saucepan of salted boiling
water until they rise to the surface: according to the
packet instructions for bought gnocchi or for 3–4
minutes if using homemade. Drain thoroughly and stir
into the sauce. Serve immediately.

For mixed cheese & herb gnocchi, omit the butter,
pancetta and sage. Bring the cream to the boil, then
stir in the fontina, Parmesan and 200 g (7 oz) cubed
dolcelatte. Remove from the heat once melted and stir
in 2 tablespoons each chopped chives and flat leaf
parsley. Season and stir into the cooked gnocchi.

beef meatballs with ribbon pasta

Serves **4**
Preparation time **20 minutes**
Cooking time **1 hour
20 minutes**

400 g (13 oz) **dried tagliatelle**
  or **fettuccine**
2 slices of **stale bread**, crusts
  removed, broken into small
  pieces
75 ml (3 fl oz) **milk**
4 tablespoons **olive oil**
6 **spring onions** or **1 small
  onion**, finely chopped
1 **garlic clove**, chopped
750 g (1½ lb) **minced beef**
2 tablespoons freshly grated
  Parmesan cheese, plus
  extra to serve
freshly grated **nutmeg**, to taste
300 ml (½ pint) **dry white
  wine**
400 g (13 oz) can **chopped
  tomatoes**
2 **bay leaves**
salt and black pepper
basil leaves, to garnish

For the meatballs, soak the bread in the milk in a large bowl. Meanwhile, heat half the oil in a frying pan over a medium heat, add the spring onions or onion and garlic and cook, stirring frequently, for 5 minutes until soft and just beginning to brown.

Add the minced meat to the bread and mix well. Add the cooked onion and garlic, the Parmesan and nutmeg and season with salt and pepper. Work together with your hands until well combined and smooth. Shape into 28 even-sized balls. Heat the remaining oil in a large, nonstick frying pan, add the meatballs, in batches, and cook over a high heat, turning frequently, until golden brown. Transfer to a shallow ovenproof dish.

Pour the wine and tomatoes into the frying pan and bring to the boil, scraping up any sediment from the base. Add the bay leaves, season with salt and pepper and boil rapidly for 5 minutes. Pour the sauce over the meatballs, cover with foil and bake in a preheated oven, 180°C (350°F), Gas Mark 4, for 1 hour, or until tender.

When the meatballs and sauce are almost ready, cook the pasta in a large saucepan of salted boiling water according to the packet instructions until al dente. Drain thoroughly and serve with the meatballs and sauce. Garnish with basil leaves and a scattering of Parmesan cheese.

For pork meatballs with walnuts, replace the beef with 750 g (1½ lb) minced pork. Grind 100 g (3½ oz) walnuts and add to the meat mixture, omitting the Parmesan, then cook as above.

tortellini with creamy ham & peas

Serves **4**
Preparation time **2 minutes**
Cooking time **8–12 minutes**

15 g (½ oz) **unsalted butter**
150 g (5 oz) shelled **peas**,
  defrosted if frozen
75 g (3 oz) **ham**, cut into
  strips
300 g (10 oz) **crème fraîche**
large pinch of freshly grated
  nutmeg
500 g (1 lb) **fresh spinach
  and ricotta** or **meat tortellini**
40 g (1½ oz) **Parmesan
  cheese**, freshly grated, plus
  extra to serve

Melt the butter in a large frying pan over a medium heat until it begins to sizzle. Add the peas and ham and cook, stirring, for 3–4 minutes if using fresh peas, or just 1 minute if using defrosted frozen peas.

Stir in the crème fraîche, add the nutmeg and season with salt and pepper. Bring to the boil and boil for 2 minutes until slightly thickened.

Cook the tortellini in a large saucepan of salted boiling water according to the packet instructions until it is al dente. Drain and toss into the creamy sauce with the Parmesan. Gently stir to combine and serve at once with a scattering of Parmesan.

For bacon & courgette tortellini, replace the ham with the same quantity of bacon strips, frying them for 4 minutes. Then add 200 g (7 oz) chopped courgette in place of the peas, and proceed as above.

prosciutto & porcini pappardelle

Serves **4**
Preparation time **10 minutes**
Cooking time **6–10 minutes**

400 g (13 oz) **dried
  pappardelle** or **homemade
  pappardelle** using 1
  quantity 3-egg Pasta Dough
  (see page 10)
2 tablespoons **olive oil**
1 **garlic clove**, crushed
250 g (8 oz) **fresh porcini
  mushrooms**, sliced
250 g (8 oz) **prosciutto slices**
150 ml (¼ pint) **whipping
  cream**
handful of **flat leaf parsley**,
  chopped
75 g (3 oz) **Parmesan
  cheese**, freshly grated
salt and black pepper

Cook the pasta in a large saucepan of salted boiling water until it is al dente: according to the packet instructions for dried pasta or for 2–3 minutes if using fresh pasta.

Meanwhile, heat the oil in a saucepan over a medium heat, add the garlic and porcini and cook, stirring frequently, for 4 minutes. Cut the prosciutto into strips, trying to keep them separate. Add to the porcini mixture with the cream and parsley and season with salt and pepper. Bring to the boil, then reduce the heat and simmer for 1 minute.

Drain the pasta, add to the sauce and toss well, using 2 spoons to mix evenly. Scatter with the Parmesan, toss well and serve immediately.

For spaghetti with dried porcini & pine nuts, soak 125 g (4 oz) dried porcini in enough hot water to cover them for 15 minutes, to rehydrate them. Drain, reserving the water, pat dry with kitchen paper and fry as above. Once the porcini has been fried, as above, add the reserved soaking water to the pan and boil until the liquid has almost evaporated. Stir in the prosciutto and cream as above. Briefly toast 2 tablespoons pine nuts in the oven and add to the sauce before combining with the cooked spaghetti.

fish & seafood

tuna, rocket & lemon conchiglie

Serves **4**

Preparation time **10 minutes**, plus marinating

Cooking time **10–12 minutes**

300 g (10 oz) **canned tuna** in olive oil, drained

4 tablespoons **extra virgin olive oil**, plus extra for drizzling

finely grated **rind of 1 unwaxed lemon**

2 **garlic cloves**, crushed

1 small **red onion**, very thinly sliced

2 tablespoons roughly chopped **flat leaf parsley**

375 g (12 oz) **dried conchiglie rigate**

75 g (3 oz) **wild rocket**

salt and black pepper

Drain the tuna and put in a large serving bowl. Break up with a fork, then stir in all the remaining ingredients, except the pasta and rocket. Season with salt and pepper, cover and leave in a cool place for at least 30 minutes for the flavours to mingle.

Meanwhile, cook the pasta in a large saucepan of salted boiling water according to the packet instructions until al dente.

Drain the pasta, then toss with the rocket into the tuna mixture. Serve immediately, with the bottle of extra virgin olive oil for anyone to drizzle a little oil on to their serving if they like.

For smoked salmon & watercress conchiglie, replace the tuna with 200 g (7 oz) smoked salmon, cut into thin strips. Use 75 g (3 oz) roughly chopped watercress instead of the rocket.

tomato & anchovy spaghetti

Serves **4**
Preparation time **10 minutes**
Cooking time **1¾ hours**

500 g (1 lb) **cherry tomatoes**, halved
75 ml (3 fl oz) **extra virgin olive oil**
2 **garlic cloves**, roughly chopped
400 g (13 oz) **dried spaghetti**
50 g (2 oz) **fresh white breadcrumbs**
8 **anchovy fillets** in oil, drained, rinsed, patted dry and roughly chopped
salt and black pepper

Arrange the tomatoes, cut-side up, in a single layer in a roasting tin lined with greaseproof paper. Drizzle lightly with the oil and scatter with half the garlic. Season lightly with salt and pepper and roast in a preheated oven, 120°C (250°F), Gas Mark ½, for 1½ hours.

Cook the pasta in a large saucepan of salted boiling water according to the packet instructions until al dente. Drain.

Meanwhile, heat the remaining oil in a large frying pan over a high heat. Add the breadcrumbs and remaining garlic and cook, stirring, until golden and crisp. Remove from the heat and stir in the anchovies, roasted tomatoes and, once ready, the pasta.

Cook, stirring, over a low heat for 30 seconds until the pasta is well coated in the sauce. Serve immediately.

For sun-dried tomato & olive spaghetti, use 150 g (5 oz) sun-blush (semi-dried) tomatoes instead of roasting your own. Heat them in the olive oil for 1–2 minutes before frying the breadcrumbs. Replace the anchovies with 50 g (2 oz) sliced olives.

pasta with monkfish & mussels

Serves **4–6**
Preparation time **20 minutes**
Cooking time **45 minutes**

500 g (1 lb) **monkfish tail**
4 tablespoons **olive oil**
1 **onion**, finely chopped
4 **garlic cloves**, finely
  chopped
500 g (1 lb) **ripe tomatoes**,
  skinned, deseeded and
  chopped
¼ teaspoon **saffron threads**
1.8 litres (3 pints) **fish stock**
375 g (12 oz) **dried fideus**
1 kg (2 lb) small **live mussels**,
  cleaned (see page 120)
salt and black pepper
garlic mayonnaise, to serve

Wash and dry the monkfish tail. Using a sharp knife, cut through the bone to produce large chunks.

Heat half the oil in a saucepan over a low heat, add the onion, garlic and tomatoes and cook, stirring occasionally, for 10 minutes. Add the monkfish, saffron threads and stock and bring to the boil. Reduce the heat and simmer gently for 5 minutes, then remove the fish with a slotted spoon and set aside. Simmer the broth gently for a further 25 minutes.

Meanwhile, heat the remaining oil in a flameproof casserole over a medium heat. Add the pasta and cook, stirring constantly, for 5 minutes until golden.

Gradually stir in the tomato broth and simmer gently, stirring, until the pasta is cooked. Add the mussels, stir well and then add the monkfish. Cook for a further 5–6 minutes until the mussels have opened and the monkfish is cooked through. Season with salt and pepper and serve with garlic mayonnaise.

For seafood pasta, replace the monkfish with 750 g (1½ lb) live clams and 500 g (1 lb) cleaned squid, cut into rings. Add to the pan with the mussels and continue with the recipe as above. Serve with spicy garlic mayonnaise, adding a good pinch each of chilli powder and paprika to the garlic mayonnaise.

lemon & chilli prawn linguine

Serves **4**

Preparation time **15 minutes**

Cooking time **10–12 minutes**

375 g (12 oz) **dried linguine**
or **spaghetti**

1 tablespoon **butter**

1 tablespoon **olive oil**

1 **garlic clove**, finely chopped

2 **spring onions**, thinly sliced

2 **fresh red chillies**, deseeded
and finely chopped

425 g (14 oz) large **raw
prawns**, peeled and tails
left intact

2 tablespoons **lemon juice**

2 tablespoons finely chopped
fresh coriander leaves, plus
extra leaves to garnish

salt and black pepper

Cook the pasta in a large saucepan of salted boiling water according to the packet instructions until al dente.

Meanwhile, melt the butter with the oil in a large frying pan over a medium heat, add the garlic, spring onions and chillies and cook, stirring, for 2–3 minutes. Increase the heat to high, add the prawns and cook, stirring, for 3–4 minutes, or until they turn pink and are just cooked through. Stir in the lemon juice and coriander, then remove from the heat.

Drain the pasta thoroughly and add to the prawn mixture. Season well with salt and pepper and toss. Serve immediately, garnished with coriander leaves.

For lemon & chilli squid, replace the raw prawns with 425 g (14 oz) cleaned squid (see page 98). Slit the squid bodies down one side and lay them flat, then score the skin with a fine criss-cross pattern. Cook, stirring, for 1–2 minutes, until just cooked.

fusilli with zesty sardines

Serves **4**

Preparation time **10 minutes**

Cooking time **35 minutes**

4 tablespoons **olive oil**

1 **onion**, thinly sliced

30 g (1 oz) **raisins**

30 g (1¼ oz) **pine nuts**

thinly sliced **rind of 1 small orange**

thinly sliced **rind of 1 unwaxed lemon**

1 tablespoon roughly chopped **dill**

1 teaspoon **fennel seeds**

1 **dried red chilli**, finely chopped

2 **garlic cloves**, peeled

150 ml (¼ pint) **dry white wine**

400 g (13 oz) **dried fusilli**

75 g (3 oz) **fresh white** or **brown breadcrumbs**

325 g (11 oz) **fresh sardine fillets**, roughly chopped

3 tablespoons roughly chopped **flat leaf parsley**

Pour half the oil into a large, heavy-based frying pan and stir in the onion, raisins and pine nuts. Add the citrus rind, dill, fennel seeds and chilli, then place the pan over a very low heat. Bruise the garlic cloves with the side of a large knife and add to the pan. Cook, stirring occasionally, for 12–15 minutes until the onion is golden and caramelized. Add the wine and boil rapidly for 2 minutes.

Cook the pasta in a large saucepan of salted boiling water according to the packet instructions until al dente. Drain, reserving a ladleful of the cooking water.

Meanwhile, spread the breadcrumbs out on a large baking sheet and drizzle with the remaining oil. Toast in a preheated oven, 220°C (425°F), Gas Mark 7, for 4–5 minutes until golden brown.

Increase the heat under the frying pan to high, add the sardines and cook, stirring, for 1–2 minutes until the fish turns opaque. Toss in the pasta and stir until well combined. Add the reserved pasta cooking water and stir until the pasta is well coated and looks silky. Remove from the heat, then stir in the toasted breadcrumbs and the parsley. Serve immediately.

For fusilli with swordfish, dice 325 g (11 oz) swordfish steak and use in place of the sardines. Replace the breadcrumbs with 75 g (3 oz) close-textured country bread cut into cubes.

squid, tomato & chilli spaghetti

Serves **4**
Preparation time **20 minutes**
Cooking time **20 minutes**

1 kg (2 lb) **raw squid**
4 tablespoons **extra virgin olive oil**, plus extra to serve
1 **fresh red chilli**, thinly sliced into rounds
500 g (1 lb) **cherry tomatoes**, halved
100 ml (3½ fl oz) **dry vermouth**
400 g (13 oz) **dried spaghetti**
15 g (½ oz) **basil leaves**
1 **garlic clove**, finely chopped
grated **rind of** ½ **unwaxed lemon**
salt

Wash the squid under cold running water. Pull the tentacles away from the body – the entrails will come out easily. Remove the clear piece of cartilage from the body cavity. Wash the body thoroughly, pulling away the pinkish membrane. Cut between the tentacles and head, discarding the head and entrails. Repeat with the remaining squid. Cut the cleaned squid bodies into rounds, dry thoroughly with kitchen paper and keep chilled and covered until required.

Heat the oil in a large frying pan over a high heat, add the chilli and tomatoes and season with salt. Cook, stirring occasionally, for 5–6 minutes until the tomatoes start to soften and look slightly charred. Pour in the vermouth and boil rapidly for 2 minutes.

Cook the pasta in a saucepan of salted boiling water according to the packet instructions until al dente. Drain.

When the pasta is almost ready, bring the tomato sauce to the boil and stir in the squid, garlic and lemon rind. Cook, stirring, for 1 minute, then toss in the pasta and stir until well combined. Scatter the basil leaves over the top and serve immediately.

For white fish & pea pasta, prepare 500 g (1 lb) white fish, such as hake, removing skin and bones. Prepare the tomato sauce as above, adding 50 g (2 oz) shelled fresh or defrosted frozen peas to the pan just before pouring in the vermouth and boiling for 2 minutes. Add the fish to the pan with the basil, garlic and lemon rind and simmer gently for 2–3 minutes.

spicy tuna, tomato & olive pasta

Serves **4**
Preparation time **10 minutes**
Cooking time **10–12 minutes**

400 g (13 oz) **dried penne** or
　rigatoni
2 tablespoons **extra virgin**
　olive oil, plus extra to serve
2 **garlic cloves**, thinly sliced
large pinch of **crushed dried**
　chillies
400 g (13 oz) **ripe tomatoes**,
　roughly chopped
50 g (2 oz) **pitted black**
　olives, roughly chopped
1 tablespoon roughly chopped
　thyme
300 g (10 oz) **canned tuna** in
　olive oil, drained
salt and black pepper

Cook the pasta in a large saucepan of salted boiling water according to packet instructions until al dente.

Meanwhile, heat the oil in a large frying pan over a medium heat and add the garlic, chillies, tomatoes, olives and thyme. Bring to the boil and simmer for 5 minutes. Break the tuna up with a fork and stir into the sauce. Simmer for 2 minutes, then season with salt and pepper.

Drain the pasta, then toss into the sauce. Serve immediately, with the bottle of extra virgin olive oil for anyone to drizzle a little oil on to their serving if they like.

For fresh tuna sauce, cut a 300 g (10 oz) tuna steak into strips and season with salt and pepper. Pan-fry in the olive oil for 2 minutes before adding the other ingredients and cooking for 5 minutes.

asparagus & anchovy spaghetti

Serves **4**
Preparation time **10 minutes**
Cooking time **10–12 minutes**

375 g (12 oz) **dried spaghetti**
375 g (12 oz) **asparagus**,
  trimmed and cut into 7 cm
  (3 inch) lengths
5 tablespoons **olive oil**
50 g (2 oz) **butter**
½ teaspoon **crushed dried
  chillies**
2 **garlic cloves**, sliced
50 g (2 oz) **anchovy fillets** in
  oil, drained and chopped
2 tablespoons **lemon juice**
75 g (3 oz) **Parmesan
  cheese**, freshly shaved
salt

Cook the pasta in a large saucepan of salted boiling water according to the packet instructions until al dente.

Meanwhile, spread the asparagus out in a roasting tray, drizzle with the oil and dot with the butter. Scatter with the chillies, garlic and anchovies and cook in a preheated oven, 200°C (400°F), Gas Mark 6, for 8 minutes until tender.

Tip the asparagus mixture and all the pan juices into a bowl. Drain the pasta, add to the bowl and toss to combine. Squeeze over the lemon juice and season with salt. Serve immediately with a scattering of Parmesan shavings.

For roast pepper & anchovy spaghetti, replace the asparagus with 2 deseeded red peppers, cut into strips. Roast in the oven and proceed as above. Serve with Parmesan.

linguine with sea bass & tomatoes

Serves **4**

Preparation time **10 minutes**

Cooking time **30 minutes**

2 **garlic cloves**, peeled

4 tablespoons **extra virgin olive oil**

¼ teaspoon **crushed dried chillies**

700 g (1 lb 7 oz) **ripe tomatoes**, roughly chopped

125 ml (4 fl oz) **dry white wine**

400 g (13 oz) **dried linguine**

375 g (12 oz) skinned **sea bass fillet**, cut into thin strips

3 tablespoons roughly chopped **flat leaf parsley**

salt

Bruise the garlic cloves with the side of a large knife. Heat the oil in a large frying pan over a low heat, add the garlic and chillies and cook, stirring occasionally, for 10 minutes. If the garlic begins to colour, simply remove the pan from the hob and leave the flavours to infuse in the heat of the pan.

Add the tomatoes and wine, season lightly with salt and bring to the boil. Reduce the heat to medium and cook for 12–15 minutes until thickened.

Meanwhile, cook the pasta in a large saucepan of salted boiling water according to the packet instructions until al dente.

When the pasta is almost ready, add the sea bass and parsley to the tomato sauce and cook for 2 minutes until the fish turns opaque.

Drain the pasta, reserving a ladleful of the cooking water. Add the pasta to the sauce and cook, stirring, for 30 seconds. Add the reserved pasta cooking water and stir until the pasta is well coated. Serve immediately.

For linguine with prawns & smoked salmon, use 250 g (8 oz) peeled cooked pawns and 100 g (3½ oz) finely shredded smoked salmon in place of the sea bass. Thaw the prawns if frozen, then heat gently in the sauce for 2 minutes. Add the smoked salmon and remove from the heat. Do not season with salt before serving as smoked salmon is salty.

tuna-layered lasagne with rocket

Serves **4**
Preparation time **10 minutes**
Cooking time **10 minutes**

8 **dried lasagne sheets**
1 tablespoon **olive oil**
1 bunch of **spring onions**,
   sliced
2 **courgettes**, diced
500 g (1 lb) **cherry tomatoes**,
   quartered
2 x 200 g (7 oz) cans **tuna** in
   water, drained
65 g (2½ oz) **wild rocket**
4 teaspoons ready-made
   green pesto
black pepper
basil leaves, to garnish

Cook the pasta sheets, in batches, in a large saucepan of salted boiling water according to the packet instructions until just al dente. Drain and return to the pan to keep warm.

Meanwhile, heat the oil in a frying pan over a medium heat, add the spring onions and courgettes and cook, stirring, for 3 minutes. Remove from the heat, add the tomatoes, tuna and rocket and gently toss together.

Place a little of the tuna mixture on 4 serving plates and top with a pasta sheet. Spoon over the remaining tuna mixture, then top with the remaining pasta sheets. Season with plenty of pepper and top with a spoonful of pesto and some basil leaves before serving.

For salmon lasagne, use 400 g (14 oz) salmon fillets. Pan-fry the fillets for 2–3 minutes on each side (depending on thickness), remove bones and skin, then flake and use in place of the tuna. For a special meal, use the homemade Classic Basil Pesto (see page 158) in place of ready-made pesto.

linguine with clams

Serves **4**

Preparation time **20 minutes**

Cooking time **25 minutes**

2 tablespoons **olive oil**

2 **garlic cloves**, thinly sliced

½ **dried red chilli**, chopped

350 g (11½ oz) **dried linguine**

1 kg (2 lb) **live clams**, cleaned
(see page 120)

2 tablespoons roughly
chopped **flat leaf parsley**

salt

extra virgin olive oil, to serve
(optional)

Heat the oil in the largest frying pan you have or a wok over a low heat. Add the garlic and chilli and leave the flavours to infuse for 10 minutes. If the garlic begins to colour, simply remove the pan from the hob and leave to infuse in the heat of the pan.

Cook the pasta in a large saucepan of salted boiling water according to the packet instructions until it is al dente.

Meanwhile, increase the heat under the frying pan, add the clams and cook, stirring, until they open. This shouldn't take longer than 4–5 minutes. Take care to cook the clams and pasta at the same time so that neither are left to overcook.

Drain the pasta, reserving a ladleful of the cooking water. Stir the pasta, reserved pasta cooking water and parsley into the clams and toss over the heat for 30 seconds, to combine all the flavours. Serve immediately with a drizzle of extra virgin olive oil, if you like.

For tomato & herb bread, to accompany the pasta, mix 2 tablespoons sundried tomato purée, 3 tablespoons olive oil and 1 teaspoon each dried oregano and rosemary. Spread over a large plain focaccia and sprinkle with 1 tablespoon freshly grated Parmesan. Bake in a preheated oven, 180°C (350°F), Gas Mark 4, for 6–8 minutes or until hot. Drizzle with extra olive oil and cut into squares to serve.

garganelli with red mullet & parma ham

Serves **4**
Preparation time **10 minutes**
Cooking time **12 minutes**

400 g (13 oz) **dried garganelli**
125 g (4 oz) **unsalted butter**
4 slices of **Parma ham**, cut into 2.5 cm (1 inch) strips
300 g (10 oz) **red mullet fillets**, cut into 2.5 cm (1 inch) pieces
10 **sage leaves**, roughly chopped
salt and black pepper

Cook the pasta in a large saucepan of salted boiling water according to the packet instructions until al dente.

Meanwhile, melt the butter in a large frying pan over a medium heat. When the butter starts to foam, add the Parma ham and cook, stirring, for 2–3 minutes. Season the red mullet with salt and pepper and add to the pan, skin-side down. Scatter with the sage and cook for 2–3 minutes until the fish is opaque all the way through. If the butter begins to colour too much, reduce the heat slightly.

Drain the pasta, reserving a ladleful of the cooking water, and toss into the frying pan with the fish. Stir gently to combine, then add the reserved pasta cooking water and stir over a medium heat until the pasta is well coated and looks silky. Serve immediately.

For lemon sole garganelli, use 300 g (10 oz) lemon sole instead of the mullet and replace the sage with 4 sprigs tarragon. Toss 50 g (2 oz) roughly chopped pitted black olives into the pasta at the last minute.

black pasta with monkfish

Serves **4**
Preparation time **10 minutes**
Cooking time **10–12 minutes**

375 g (12 oz) **dried black
    squid ink pasta**
25 g (1 oz) **butter**
200 g (7 oz) **monkfish tail**,
    cut into 2.5 cm (1 inch)
    cubes
2 large **fresh red chillies**,
    deseeded and finely
    chopped
2 **garlic cloves**, chopped
2 tablespoons **Thai fish
    sauce**
150 g (5 oz) **baby spinach**
juice of 2 limes
salt
lime wedges, to serve

Cook the pasta in a large saucepan of salted boiling water according to the packet instructions until al dente. Drain thoroughly and return to the pan. Add the butter and toss to coat.

Meanwhile, put the monkfish cubes on a large piece of foil and top with the chillies, garlic and fish sauce. Fold up the edges of the foil and turn them over to seal the parcel. Place on a baking sheet and cook in a preheated oven, 200°C (400°F), Gas Mark 6, for 8–10 minutes until cooked through.

Toss the contents of the parcel with the hot pasta. Add the spinach and stir until it wilts. Add the lime juice and season with salt, then serve the pasta immediately with lime wedges.

For black pasta with prawns & scallops, use 300 g (10 oz) peeled raw tiger pawns and 8 scallops, halved and with coral removed. Cook in the butter with the chillies and garlic, omitting the fish sauce, for about 3 minutes, turning the scallops after 1–2 minutes. Combine with the pasta and finish as above.

king prawn & courgette linguine

Serves **4**
Preparation time **10 minutes**
Cooking time **10–12 minutes**

400 g (13 oz) **dried linguine**
3 tablespoons **olive oil**
200 g (7 oz) peeled **raw king prawns**
2 **garlic cloves**, crushed
finely grated **rind of 1 unwaxed lemon**
1 **fresh red chilli**, deseeded and finely chopped
400 g (13 oz) **courgettes**, coarsely grated
50 g (2 oz) **unsalted butter**, cut into cubes
salt

Cook the pasta in a large saucepan of salted boiling water according to the packet instructions until al dente. Drain.

Meanwhile, heat the oil in a large frying pan over a high heat until the surface of the oil seems to shimmer slightly. Add the prawns, garlic, lemon rind and chilli, season with salt and cook, stirring, for 2 minutes until the prawns turn pink. Add the courgettes and butter, season with a little more salt and stir well. Cook, stirring, for 30 seconds.

Toss in the pasta and stir until the butter has melted and all the ingredients are well combined. Serve immediately.

For squid & pumpkin sauce, replace the prawns with 200 g (7 oz) prepared squid rings and the courgette with 400 g (13 oz) coarsely grated pumpkin, and cook as described above.

tagliatelle with spicy tuna steak

Serves **4**
Preparation time **15 minutes**
Cooking time **10–12 minutes**

375 g (12 oz) **dried green tagliatelle**
2 large **fresh green chillies**, deseeded and roughly chopped
25 g (1 oz) **fresh coriander with roots**
1 large **garlic clove**, roughly chopped
25 g (1 oz) **almonds**, toasted
2 tablespoons **lime juice**
5 tablespoons **olive oil**
4 **tuna steaks**, about 150 g (5 oz) each
salt
lime wedges, to serve

Cook the pasta in a large saucepan of salted boiling water according to the packet instructions until al dente.

Meanwhile, put the chillies, coriander, garlic, almonds and lime juice in a food processor and process for 10 seconds. With the motor running, drizzle in the oil. Season with salt.

Heat a ridged griddle pan or heavy-based frying pan over a high heat until smoking. Add the tuna steaks and cook for 30 seconds on each side, or until seared but still pink in the middle. Remove from the pan and slice in half.

Drain the pasta thoroughly, then toss with two-thirds of the coriander sauce and divide between 4 serving plates. Top each portion with 2 pieces of tuna and a dollop of the remaining sauce. Serve with some lime wedges.

For tagliatelle with spicy salmon, cook 150 g (5 oz) salmon steaks until charred and firm. As with the tuna, you need a very hot pan for searing and exact cooking times will depend on the thickness of the steaks. Serve with cucumber salad, made by combining 1 large cucumber, peeled and sliced, with 2 tablespoons snipped chives and 2 tablespoons plain yogurt.

crab linguine with chilli

Serves **4**
Preparation time **10 minutes**
Cooking time **10–12 minutes**

400 g (13 oz) **dried linguine**
100 ml (3½ fl oz) **extra virgin olive oil**
1 **fennel bulb**, trimmed and cut into thin strips
1 **fresh red chilli**, finely chopped
2 **garlic cloves**, thinly sliced
300 g (10 oz) **fresh crabmeat**
100 ml (3½ fl oz) **dry vermouth**, such as Noilly Prat
juice of 1 lemon
3 tablespoons roughly chopped **flat leaf parsley**
fennel fronds, to garnish
salt

Cook the pasta in a large saucepan of salted boiling water according to the packet instructions until al dente.

Meanwhile, heat 2 tablespoons of the oil in a large frying pan over a low heat, add the fennel, chilli and garlic and cook, stirring occasionally, for 5–6 minutes until slightly softened. Stir in the crabmeat, increase the heat to high and pour in the vermouth. Boil rapidly for 1–2 minutes until most of the liquid has evaporated, then remove from the heat and stir in the remaining oil and the lemon juice. Season with salt.

Drain the pasta and stir into the sauce with the parsley. Garnish with fennel fronds and serve immediately.

For crab & pasta salad, combine the ingredients, except the vermouth. Use an unwaxed lemon and add its grated rind. Use 300 g (10 oz) small pasta shells. When the pasta is cooked, drain, rinse under cold water and drain again. Toss the sauce in the pasta and add a little extra olive oil, if needed. Serve on 1 shredded iceberg lettuce.

shellfish with oil, garlic & chilli

Serves **4**

Preparation time **20 minutes**, plus soaking

Cooking time **25 minutes**

750 g (1½ lb) **live clams**

750 g (1½ lb) **live mussels**

75 ml (3 fl oz) **extra virgin olive oil**

2 **garlic cloves**, thinly sliced

½ **dried red chilli**, chopped

375 g (12 oz) **dried spaghetti**

150 ml (¼ pint) **dry white wine**

2 tablespoons roughly chopped **flat leaf parsley**

Wash the clams and mussels under cold running water, discarding any that are broken or that remain open when tapped. Pull away the 'beards' from the mussels and scrub well. Soak the clams and mussels in plenty of cold water for 30 minutes, then drain and rinse again in cold running water. Put in a bowl, cover with a wet tea towel and refrigerate until required.

Heat the oil in the largest frying pan you have or a wok over a low heat. Add the garlic and chilli and leave the flavours to infuse for 10 minutes. If the garlic begins to colour, simply remove the pan from the hob and leave to infuse in the heat of the pan.

Cook the pasta in a large saucepan of salted boiling water according to the packet instructions until al dente.

Meanwhile, increase the heat under the frying pan. Add the wine and boil rapidly for 2 minutes. Add the clams and mussels and cook, stirring, until they open. This shouldn't take longer than 4–5 minutes.

Drain the pasta and add to the frying pan with the parsley. Toss over the heat for 30 seconds, to combine all the flavours. Serve immediately.

For tomato, garlic & chilli sauce, halve 250 g (8 oz) cherry tomatoes and cook them, cut-side down, in the oil with the garlic and chilli. Serve with the shellfish, or omit the shellfish and add 100 g (3½ oz) chopped rocket instead.

farfalle with smoked salmon & roe

Serves **4**

Preparation time **10 minutes**

Cooking time **25 minutes**

40 g (1½ oz) **unsalted butter**
1 tablespoon **olive oil**
2 **shallots**, thinly sliced
150 ml (¼ pint) **dry white wine**
200 g (7 oz) **crème fraîche**
125 g (4 oz) **smoked salmon**, roughly cut into strips
400 g (13 oz) **dried farfalle**
2 tablespoons roughly chopped **dill**
30 g (1¼ oz) **salmon roe**
salt and black pepper

Melt the butter in a large frying pan over a low heat. Add the oil and shallots and cook, stirring occasionally, for 6–7 minutes until softened. Pour in the wine, increase the heat to high and boil rapidly for 2–3 minutes until reduced by half. Remove from the heat and stir in the crème fraîche and salmon strips. Season with salt and plenty of pepper.

Cook the pasta in a large saucepan of salted boiling water according to the packet instructions until al dente. Drain, reserving a ladleful of the cooking water.

Bring the pasta sauce to a slow simmer, then add the pasta and stir until well combined. Add the reserved cooking water from the pasta and continue stirring until the pasta is well coated and looks silky. Gently toss in the dill and roe, and serve immediately.

For farfalle with smoked salmon, spinach, rocket & asparagus, toss 75 g (3 oz) baby spinach and wild rocket into the pasta with the sauce. Cook 150 g (5 oz) asparagus tips with the pasta for the last 3 minutes of the cooking time. Omit the salmon roe.

lobster sauce with spaghetti

Serves **6**
Preparation time **10 minutes**
Cooking time **25 minutes**

3 **shell-on lobsters**, weighing
   about 400 g (13 oz) each
600 g (1 lb 2 oz) **dried**
   spaghetti
3 tablespoons **olive oil**
2–3 **garlic cloves**, chopped
large pinch of **crushed dried**
   chillies
1 glass **dry white wine**
1 tablespoon chopped
   parsley, plus extra to garnish
salt and black pepper

Bring a large saucepan of salted water to the boil, drop in 1 lobster and simmer for 12 minutes. Leave to cool, then remove the lobster flesh from the shell.

Cook the pasta in a large saucepan of salted boiling water according to the packet instructions until al dente.

Meanwhile, split the other 2 lobsters in half lengthways, remove and discard the stomach sacs, then chop into large pieces, legs, head and all.

Heat the oil in a sauté pan, add the garlic, chillies and chopped lobster and cook, stirring, for 2 minutes. Add the wine and bring to the boil. Add the boiled lobster meat and stir in the parsley. Season with salt and pepper.

Drain the pasta and toss with the lobster mixture. Serve immediately, garnished with parsley. Eat the lobster from the shells with your fingers – sucking the shells is part of the enjoyment!

For prawn sauce with spaghetti, omit the lobster and add 250 g (8 oz) raw peeled prawns to the pan with the garlic and chillies. Cook, stirring, for 2–3 minutes until the prawns are pink, then add the wine as above.

fusilli with swordfish & artichoke

Serves **4**
Preparation time **5 minutes**,
 plus marinating
Cooking time **12–15 minutes**

juice of ½ **lemon**
2 **garlic cloves**, thinly sliced
1 **fresh red chilli**, deseeded
 and finely chopped
100 ml (3¹/₂ fl oz) **extra virgin
 olive oil**
400 g (13 oz) **swordfish
 steak**, cut into 1½ cm
 (¾ inch) cubes
375 g (12 oz) **dried fusilli**
200 g (7 oz) **bottled or
 canned artichoke hearts** in
 olive oil, drained
50 g (2 oz) **pitted black
 olives**, roughly chopped
3 tablespoons roughly
 chopped **mint**
salt

Put the lemon juice, garlic, chilli and 2 tablespoons of the oil in a non-metallic bowl. Add the swordfish cubes and turn to coat in the marinade. Cover and leave to marinate in a cool place for 15 minutes.

Cook the pasta in a large saucepan of salted boiling water according to the packet instructions until al dente.

Meanwhile, heat the remaining oil in a large frying pan over a high heat. Cut the artichokes in half, add to the pan with the olives and cook, stirring, for 2 minutes. Season the swordfish with salt and add to the pan with the marinade. Cook for 2–3 minutes, stirring occasionally, until the fish is just cooked.

Drain the pasta, reserving a ladleful of the cooking water. Stir into the frying pan and add the mint. Toss well over a low heat and pour in the reserved pasta cooking water. Continue stirring until the pasta is well coated and looks silky. Serve immediately.

For seafood & artichoke sauce, use 250 g (8 oz) peeled raw prawns or squid rings, or a combination of both. Cook until the prawns turn pink or the squid is firm and opaque.

smoked trout & herb butter linguine

Serves **4**
Preparation time **10 minutes**
Cooking time **10–12 minutes**

400 g (13 oz) **dried linguine**
125 g (4 oz) **unsalted butter**
300 g (10 oz) **hot smoked
    trout**, flaked
5 **spring onions**, finely sliced
1 tablespoon roughly chopped
    tarragon
4 tablespoons snipped **chives**
4 tablespoons chopped **flat
    leaf parsley**
juice of 1 lemon
salt and black pepper

Cook the pasta in a large saucepan of salted boiling water according to the packet instructions until al dente.

Meanwhile, melt the butter in a saucepan over a low heat. Stir in all the remaining ingredients and remove from the heat.

Drain the pasta, reserving a ladleful of the cooking water. Toss the pasta into the butter and herb mixture and season with salt and pepper. If the pasta looks dry, stir in some of the reserved pasta cooking water to give it a light, silky coating of sauce. Serve immediately.

For spicy horseradish topping, stir 2 tablespoons horseradish cream into 150 ml (¼ pint) crème fraîche. Season with black pepper. Top each pasta portion with a dollop of the avocado mixture.

macaroni & haddock cheese

Serves **4**
Preparation time **2 minutes**
Cooking time **30 minutes**

600 ml (1 pint) **milk**
325 g (11 oz) **undyed smoked haddock fillets**
325 g (11 oz) **dried macaroni**
50 g (2 oz) **unsalted butter**, plus extra for greasing
25 g (1 oz) **plain flour**
1 tablespoon **wholegrain mustard**
250 ml (8 fl oz) **single cream**
125 g (4 oz) shelled **peas**, thawed if frozen
125 g (4 oz) **Cheddar cheese**, grated
4 tablespoons freshly grated **Parmesan cheese**
1 tablespoon roughly chopped **flat leaf parsley**
125 g (4 oz) coarse **fresh white** or **brown breadcrumbs**
1 tablespoon **olive oil**
salt and black pepper

Heat the milk in a wide-based, shallow saucepan to scalding point (it should barely shiver). Add the haddock, in a single layer, and poach gently for 6–8 minutes until the flesh flakes easily. Lift the fish from the pan with a slotted spoon. Remove the skin and break the flesh into large flakes. Strain the milk into a jug.

Cook the pasta in a large saucepan of salted boiling water according to the packet instructions until al dente.

Meanwhile, melt the butter in a saucepan over a very low heat. Add the flour and cook, stirring, for 2 minutes until it is a light biscuity colour. Remove from the heat and slowly add the reserved milk, stirring away lumps. Return to the heat and simmer, stirring, for 2–3 minutes until creamy. Stir in the mustard, cream, peas, Cheddar and half the Parmesan. Season with salt and pepper.

Drain the pasta and return to the pan. Fold the sauce and haddock flakes into the pasta and transfer to a greased ovenproof dish. Mix the parsley and remaining Parmesan into the breadcrumbs and scatter evenly over the pasta. Drizzle with the oil and bake in a preheated oven, 220°C (425°F), Gas Mark 7, for 10 minutes until bubbling and golden.

For tarragon carrots, as a side dish, halve 250–300 g (8–10 oz) baby carrots and blanch in boiling water for 2 minutes. Drain and cook, with the lid on the pan, in 25 g (1 oz) butter, 1 tablespoon olive oil and 1 teaspoon sugar, for 5 minutes until tender. Add 2 tablespoons chopped tarragon before serving.

pasta with scallops & pancetta

Serves **4**
Preparation time **15 minutes**
Cooking time **15–20 minutes**

5 tablespoons **extra virgin olive oil**
125 g (4 oz) **pancetta**, cut into cubes
1 **fresh red chilli**, deseeded and finely chopped
2 **garlic cloves**, thinly sliced
250 g (8 oz) **raw shelled scallops**
400 g (13 oz) **dried linguine**
100 ml (3½ fl oz) **dry white wine**
2 tablespoons roughly chopped **flat leaf parsley**
salt

Heat the oil in a large frying pan over a medium heat, add the pancetta and cook, stirring occasionally, for 4–5 minutes until golden and crisp. Remove from the heat and stir in the chilli and garlic. Leave the flavours to infuse while you prepare the scallops and start cooking the pasta.

If you have bought scallops with the orange roe, carefully separate the roe from the main body of the scallops. Using a small, sharp knife, slice once across the thickness of each scallop to make thinner discs. Set aside.

Cook the pasta in a large saucepan of salted boiling water according to packet instructions until al dente.

When the pasta is almost ready, heat the frying pan with the pancetta over a high heat. When the oil starts to sizzle, season the scallops and roes with salt, add to the pan and cook, stirring gently, for 2 minutes. Pour in the wine and boil rapidly for 2 minutes.

Drain the pasta and stir into the frying pan with the parsley. Toss the pasta over the heat for 30 seconds, to combine all the flavours. Serve immediately.

For pasta with asparagus, scallops & pancetta, simply add 150 g (5 oz) asparagus tips to the pasta cooking water for the last 3 minutes of the cooking time and complete the recipe as above.

vegetarian

quickest-ever tomato pasta sauce

Serves **4**
Preparation time **2 minutes**
Cooking time **10–12 minutes**

400 g (13 oz) **dried pasta** of
  your choice
2 tablespoons **olive oil**
2 **garlic cloves**, finely
  chopped
500 ml (17 fl oz) **passata
  (sieved tomatoes)**
25 g (1 oz) **unsalted butter**
  (optional)
salt and black pepper
freshly grated **Parmesan
  cheese** or **extra virgin olive
  oil**, to serve

Cook the pasta in a large saucepan of salted boiling water according to the packet instructions until al dente.

Meanwhile, heat the olive oil in a saucepan over a low heat, then add the garlic and cook, stirring, for 30 seconds. Increase the heat to high and quickly stir in the passata. Bring to the boil and season with salt and pepper, then reduce the heat and simmer for 5 minutes. Remove from the heat.

Drain the pasta thoroughly, then stir into the sauce. If you want a more delicate, sweet flavour, add the butter and toss until melted. Serve immediately with a drizzle of extra virgin olive oil or a scattering of grated Parmesan.

For tomato sauce with olives & basil, make the sauce as above, adding a large pinch of crushed dried chillies and 1 teaspoon dried oregano with the garlic. Simmer for 30 minutes: the key to tomato sauce is either to barely cook it (as above), so that the acidity from the tomatoes isn't released, or cook it for a long period, to cook off the acidity. Before serving, stir in 50 g (2 oz) chopped black olives together with 10 torn basil leaves.

spaghetti with capers & lemon

Serves **4**
Preparation time **5 minutes**
Cooking time **10–12 minutes**

400 g (13 oz) **dried spaghetti**
150 ml (¼ pint) **extra virgin olive oil**
2 large **garlic cloves**, thinly sliced
1 **fresh red chilli**, deseeded and finely chopped
2½ tablespoons **capers** in brine, rinsed and drained
finely pared **rind of 1 unwaxed lemon**
salt

Cook the pasta in a large saucepan of salted boiling water according to the packet instructions until al dente.

Meanwhile, pour the oil into a large frying pan, add all the remaining ingredients and place over a very low heat. Leave the flavours to infuse for 5 minutes. If the garlic begins to colour, simply remove the pan from the hob and leave to infuse in the heat of the pan.

Drain the pasta, add to the frying pan and toss with the oil mixture. Serve immediately.

For spaghetti with capers, pine nuts & green olives, proceed as above, adding 100 g (3½ oz) chopped green olives to the pan with the other ingredients. Combine the sauce and the pasta as above and sprinkle with 2 tablespoons pine nuts before serving.

veggie carbonara

Serves **4**
Preparation time **5 minutes**
Cooling time **15 minutes**

2 tablespoons **olive oil**
2 **garlic cloves**, finely
   chopped
3 **courgettes**, thinly sliced
6 **spring onions**, cut into
   1 cm (½ inch) lengths
400 g (13 oz) **dried penne**
4 **egg yolks**
100 ml (3½ fl oz) **crème
   fraîche**
75 g (3 oz) freshly grated
   Parmesan cheese, plus
   extra to serve
salt and black pepper

Heat the oil in a heavy-based frying pan over a medium-high heat. Add the garlic, courgettes and spring onions and cook, stirring, for 4–5 minutes until the courgettes are tender. Set aside.

Cook the pasta in a large saucepan of salted boiling water according to the packet instructions until al dente.

Meanwhile, crack the egg yolks into a bowl and season with salt and a generous grinding of pepper. Mix together with a fork.

Just before the pasta is ready, return the pan with the courgette mixture to the heat. Stir in the crème fraîche and bring to the boil.

Drain the pasta thoroughly, return it to the pan and immediately stir in the egg mixture, Parmesan and the creamy courgette mixture. Stir vigorously and serve immediately with a scattering of grated Parmesan.

For asparagus carbonara, replace the courgettes with 250 g (8 oz) asparagus spears. Cut the spears into 2.5 cm (1 inch) lengths and cook in exactly the same way as the courgettes.

courgette & gremolata linguine

Serves **4**
Preparation time **15 minutes**
Cooking time **12 minutes**

2 tablespoons **olive oil**
6 large **courgettes**, thickly
   sliced
8 **spring onions**, finely sliced
400 g (13 oz) **dried linguine**
fresh **Parmesan cheese
   shavings**, to serve

Gremolata
finely grated **rind of
   2 unwaxed lemons**
1 tablespoon **olive oil**
10 tablespoons chopped **flat
   leaf parsley**
2 **garlic cloves**, crushed

First make the gremolata. Mix all the ingredients together in a bowl.

Heat the oil in a nonstick frying pan over a high heat, add the courgettes and cook, stirring frequently, for 10 minutes, or until browned. Add the spring onions and cook, stirring, for 1–2 minutes.

Meanwhile, cook the pasta in a large saucepan of boiling water according to the packet instructions until al dente.

Drain the pasta thoroughly and tip into a serving bowl. Add the courgette mixture and the gremolata and toss well. Serve immediately with a scattering of Parmesan shavings.

For green bean linguine with an oriental gremolata, use finely grated lime rind in place of the lemon rind and fresh coriander instead of the parsley in the gremolata. Omit the courgettes and replace them with 300 g (10 oz) fine green beans, cut into 2.5 cm (1 inch) lengths. Boil for 3–5 minutes. Fry the drained beans and the spring onions for 1 minute.

no-cook-tomato spaghetti

Serves **4**

Preparation time **10 minutes,**
plus standing

Cooking time **10–12 minutes**

750 g (1½ lb) **very ripe
tomatoes,** quartered

2 **garlic cloves,** peeled

10 **basil leaves**

2 teaspoons **fennel seeds**

5 tablespoons **extra virgin
olive oil**

400 g (13 oz) **dried spaghetti**

2 x 150 g (5 oz) **buffalo
mozzarella cheese balls,**
cut into cubes

salt and black pepper

Put the tomatoes, garlic cloves and basil in a food processor and process until the tomatoes are finely chopped but not smooth. Transfer to a large bowl and add the fennel seeds and oil. Season with salt and pepper. Leave the flavours to infuse for at least 15 minutes before cooking the pasta.

Cook the pasta in a large saucepan of salted boiling water according to the packet instructions until al dente. Drain, stir into the prepared tomato sauce, then toss in the mozzarella. Serve immediately.

For herby no-cook tomato orechiette, replace 125 g (4 oz) of the tomatoes with sun-blush (semi-dried) tomatoes. Coarsely shred 150 g (5 oz) rocket and mix with the leaves from 4 sprigs of thyme. Toss with the cooked orechiette and serve with mozzarella, as above.

wild mushroom pappardelle

Serves **4**
Preparation time **15 minutes**
Cooking time **12–25 minutes**

375 g (12 oz) **mixed wild mushrooms**, cleaned
6 tablespoons **olive oil**
1 **garlic clove**, thinly sliced
1 **fresh red chilli**, deseeded and finely chopped
juice of ½ **lemon**
3 tablespoons roughly chopped **flat leaf parsley**
50 g (2 oz) **unsalted butter**, cut into cubes
400 g (13 oz) **dried pappardelle** or **homemade pappardelle** using 1 quantity 3-egg Pasta Dough (see page 10)
salt and black pepper
fresh **Parmesan cheese shavings**, to serve

Trim the mushrooms, slicing porcini mushrooms (if you can find some fresh) and tearing large delicate mushrooms, such as chantarelles or oyster mushrooms.

Heat the oil in a large, heavy-based frying pan over a low heat. Add the garlic and chilli and leave the flavours to infuse for 5 minutes. If the garlic begins to colour, simply remove the pan from the hob and leave to infuse in the heat of the pan.

Increase the heat to high, add the mushrooms and cook, stirring, for 3–4 minutes until the mushrooms are tender and golden. Remove from the heat and stir in the lemon juice, parsley and butter. Season with salt and pepper.

Cook the pasta in a large saucepan of salted boiling water until it is al dente: according to the packet instructions for dried pasta or for 2–3 minutes if using fresh pasta. Drain thoroughly, reserving a ladleful of the cooking water.

Return the pan with the mushroom mixture to a medium heat and stir in the pasta. Toss until well combined, then pour in the reserved pasta cooking water and continue stirring until the pasta is well coated. Serve immediately with Parmesan shavings.

For mild & creamy mushroom pappardelle, omit the chilli, halve the quantity of oil and stir 200 g (7 oz) crème fraîche into the mushrooms with the butter. Bring to the boil before removing from the heat, then continue with the recipe as above. Drizzle with 2 teaspoons truffle oil before serving.

roasted tomato & ricotta pasta

Serves **4**
Preparation time **10 minutes**
Cooking time **15–20 minutes**

500 g (1 lb) **cherry tomatoes**,
  halved
4 tablespoons **extra virgin
  olive oil**
2 teaspoons chopped **thyme
  leaves**
4 **garlic cloves**, sliced
pinch of **crushed dried
  chillies**
400 g (13 oz) **dried pasta**
1 bunch of **basil leaves**, torn
125 g (4 oz) **ricotta cheese**,
  crumbled
salt and black pepper

Put the tomatoes in a roasting tin with the oil, thyme, garlic and chillies, and season with salt and pepper. Roast in a preheated oven, 200°C (400°F), Gas Mark 6, for 15–20 minutes until the tomatoes have softened and released their juices.

Meanwhile, cook the pasta in a large saucepan of salted boiling water according to the packet instructions until al dente. Drain and return to the pan.

Stir the tomatoes with all their pan juices and most of the basil leaves into the pasta and toss gently until combined. Season with salt and pepper and spoon into serving bowls.

Chop the remaining basil, mix into the ricotta and season with salt and pepper. Spoon into a small dish for guests to spoon on to the pasta.

For roasted tomato & goats' cheese sauce, replace the ricotta with 125 g (4 oz) crumbly goats' cheese. This piquant, herb-scented dish goes well with pasta verde, spinach-flavoured pasta shapes.

individual macaroni cheeses

Serves **4**
Preparation time **10 minutes**
Cooking time **20 minutes**

250 g (8 oz) **dried macaroni**
125 g (4 oz) **mushrooms**,
   sliced
1 **garlic clove**, crushed
150 ml (¼ pint) **single cream**
150 ml (¼ pint) **milk**
pinch of freshly grated
   nutmeg
175 g (6 oz) **hard cheese,**
   such as Cheddar or Gruyère,
   grated
4 tablespoons chopped **basil**
salt and black pepper

Cook the pasta in a large saucepan of salted boiling water according to the packet instructions until al dente.

Meanwhile, heat a small, dry frying pan over a medium heat, add the mushrooms and cook, stirring, for 5 minutes. Add the garlic and cook, stirring, for 1 minute. Add the cream, milk and nutmeg and bring just to boiling point.

Stir in 125 g (4 oz) of the cheese and all the basil, remove from the heat and stir until the cheese has melted. Season with salt and pepper.

Drain the pasta and tip into a large bowl. Add the sauce and stir well to combine.

Spoon into individual gratin dishes, top with the remaining cheese and bake in a preheated oven, 230°C (450°F), Gas Mark 8, for 10 minutes until golden brown. Serve immediately.

For macaroni cheese with spinach & walnuts, add 250 g (8 oz) frozen spinach with the garlic and stir fry until thawed. Proceed as above, stirring in 4 tablespoons chopped walnuts before spooning into individual dishes, topping with cheese and baking.

broad bean & asparagus penne

Serves **4**
Preparation time **10 minutes**
Cooking time **12–15 minutes**

300 g (10 oz) **dried penne**
500 g (1 lb) **asparagus**,
   trimmed and cut into short
   lengths
4 tablespoons **olive oil**
250 g (8 oz) shelled **fresh
   broad beans** or **peas**
75 ml (3 fl oz) **double cream**
75 g (3 oz) **Parmesan
   cheese**, freshly grated, plus
   extra to serve
4 tablespoons chopped **mint**
salt and black pepper

Cook the pasta in a large saucepan of salted boiling water according to the packet instructions until al dente.

Meanwhile, spread the asparagus out on a baking sheet, brush generously with oil and season with salt and pepper. Place under a preheated hot grill and cook for 8 minutes, turning as they brown.

Cook the beans or peas in a separate saucepan of lightly salted boiling water for 2 minutes, then drain.

Drain the pasta. Pour the cream into the empty pasta pan over the heat, add the cooked beans or peas, the grilled asparagus and the Parmesan and season with salt and pepper. Return the cooked pasta to the pan, add the mint and toss well with 2 wooden spoons. Serve immediately with a scattering of Parmesan.

For penne with chargrilled asparagus & almonds, heat a ridged griddle pan over a high heat and brush with olive oil, add the asparagus in a single layer and cook, turning occasionally and brushing with a little more oil, until lightly charred all over and just tender. Omit the beans and mint. Brown 50 g (2 oz) slivered almonds in the pan, before adding the cream, asparagus, Parmesan and salt and pepper. Combine with the pasta before serving.

orecchiette with walnut sauce

Serves **4**
Preparation time **5 minutes**
Cooking time **10–12 minutes**

375 g (12 oz) **dried orecchiette**
50 g (2 oz) **butter**
15 **sage leaves**, roughly chopped
2 **garlic cloves**, finely chopped
125 g (5 oz) **walnuts**, finely chopped
150 ml (¼ pint) **single cream**
65 g (2½ oz) **Parmesan cheese**, freshly grated
salt and black pepper

Cook the pasta in a large saucepan of salted boiling water according to the packet instructions until al dente.

Meanwhile, melt the butter in a frying pan over a medium heat. When it begins to foam and sizzle, stir in the sage and garlic and cook, stirring, for 1–2 minutes until golden. Remove from the heat and stir in the walnuts, cream and Parmesan.

Drain the pasta and stir it thoroughly into the sauce. Season with salt and pepper and serve immediately.

For spinach, spring onion & avocado salad, to serve with the pasta, use 150 g (5 oz) baby spinach leaves, 4 finely sliced spring onions and 2 peeled, stoned and sliced avocados. Toss together and spoon into separate side dishes.

porcini & tomato tagliatelle

Serves **4**
Preparation time **10 minutes**,
   plus soaking
Cooking time **35 minutes**

25 g (1 oz) **dried porcini
   mushrooms**
200 ml (7 fl oz) **boiling water**
2 tablespoons **olive oil**
2 **garlic cloves,** finely
   chopped
2 tablespoons roughly
   chopped **thyme**
2 x 400 g (13 oz) cans
   cherry tomatoes or
   chopped tomatoes
400 g (13 oz) **dried
   tagliatelle** or **homemade
   tagliatelle** using 1 quantity
   3-egg Pasta Dough (see
   page 10)
40 g (1½ oz) **unsalted butter,**
   cut into cubes
salt and black pepper
freshly grated **Parmesan
   cheese,** to serve (optional)

Soak the porcini in the measurement water for about
10 minutes. Drain, reserving the soaking water, and
squeeze out any excess water.

Heat the oil in a heavy-based frying pan, add the garlic
and thyme and stir for 30 seconds. Increase the heat
to high. Add the porcini, season with salt and pepper
and stir for 1 minute. Pour in the reserved soaking
water and the tomatoes. Bring to the boil, reduce the
heat to very low and simmer, uncovered, for 30 minutes
until thickened, adding a little water if the sauce begins
to stick. Adjust the seasoning.

When the sauce is almost ready, cook the pasta in a
large saucepan of salted boiling water until al dente:
according to the packet instructions for dried pasta or
for 2 minutes if using fresh pasta. Drain thoroughly,
reserving a ladleful of the cooking water.

Return the pasta to the pan and place over a low heat.
Stir in the mushroom sauce and the butter and mix
together thoroughly. Add the reserved pasta cooking
water and continue stirring for a few seconds until the
pasta is well coated and looks silky. Serve immediately
with a scattering of grated Parmesan, if liked.

For broccoli & tomato tagliatelle, omit the porcini
and instead cut 250 g (8 oz) broccoli into small
florets. Boil for 2 minutes, then drain well. Make the
tomato sauce as above (omitting the soaking water),
then combine the sauce and broccoli with the butter
and pasta as described above.

classic basil pesto

Serves **4**
Preparation time **2 minutes**
Cooking time **10–12 minutes**

400 g (13 oz) **dried trofie**
75 g (3 oz) **basil leaves**
50 g (2 oz) **pine nuts**
2 **garlic cloves**
50 g (2 oz) **Parmesan cheese**, freshly grated, plus extra to serve
100 ml (3½ fl oz) **olive oil**
salt and black pepper
basil leaves, to garnish

Cook the pasta in a large saucepan of salted boiling water according to the packet instructions until al dente.

Meanwhile, put the basil, pine nuts and garlic in a food processor and process until well blended. Transfer to a bowl and stir in the Parmesan and oil. Season with salt and pepper.

Drain the pasta, reserving a ladleful of the cooking water, and return to the pan. Stir in the pesto, adding enough of the reserved pasta cooking water to loosen the mixture. Serve immediately with a scattering of grated Parmesan and garnished with basil leaves.

For potato & bean pesto pasta, the classic Genovese way of serving pesto, start by cooking 250 g (8 oz) peeled and sliced potatoes in a large saucepan of salted boiling water for 5 minutes, then add the pasta and cook according to the packet instructions until al dente. When there are 5 minutes of the cooking time remaining, add 150 g (5 oz) trimmed French beans to the pan. After draining the pasta, stir in the pesto as above. A long pasta shape such as linguine suits this variation better.

goats' cheese & watercress pesto

Serves **4**
Preparation time **10 minutes**
Cooking time **10–12 minutes**

375 g (12 oz) **dried fusilli**
50 g (2 oz) **pine nuts**,
 toasted, plus extra to serve
1 **garlic clove**, roughly
 chopped
150 g (5 oz) **watercress**, plus
 extra sprigs to serve
7 tablespoons **extra virgin
 olive oil**
150 g (5 oz) **crumbly goats'
 cheese**, plus extra to serve
salt and black pepper

Cook the pasta in a large saucepan of salted boiling water according to the packet instructions until al dente.

Meanwhile, put the pine nuts, garlic and watercress in a food processor with a generous pinch of salt. Process for 15 seconds until roughly chopped. Then, with the motor running, drizzle in the oil while you process for a further 20 seconds.

Drain the pasta thoroughly and tip into a bowl. Crumble in the goats' cheese and stir well. Season with pepper, then stir the pesto into the hot pasta. Divide between 4 serving plates and serve immediately with a scattering of goats' cheese and pine nuts and some watercress sprigs.

For goats' cheese and rocket pesto, replace the watercress with 150 g (5 oz) wild rocket. Be careful not to over-blend the watercress (or rocket) and pine nuts as the pesto is best when it retains some texture.

radicchio & cheese crumb pasta

Serves **2**
Preparation time **10 minutes**
Cooking time **13 minutes**

175 g (6 oz) **dried spaghetti**
65 g (2½ oz) **butter**
25 g (1 oz) **fresh white breadcrumbs**
15 g (½ oz) **Parmesan cheese**, freshly grated
2 **shallots**, finely chopped
1 **garlic clove**, sliced
1 head of **radicchio**, shredded
dash of **lemon juice**
salt and black pepper

Cook the pasta in a large saucepan of salted boiling water according to the packet instructions until it is al dente.

Meanwhile, melt half the butter in a frying pan, add the breadcrumbs and cook, stirring frequently, for 5 minutes until golden and crisp. Transfer the crumbs to a bowl and leave to cool slightly then stir in the Parmesan cheese.

Melt the remaining butter in a large saucepan or wok over a low heat, add the shallots and garlic and cook, stirring occasionally, for 5 minutes, or until softened. Add the radicchio and lemon juice and season with salt and pepper. Cook, stirring, for 2 minutes, or until the radicchio has wilted.

Drain the pasta, reserving 2 tablespoons of the cooking water. Add the pasta and the reserved cooking water to the radicchio mixture and toss briefly over the heat. Serve immediately is small serving bowls, topped with the cheese crumbs.

For spinach & smoked cheese crumb pasta, replace the radicchio with 250 g (8 oz) spinach and use grated smoked cheese instead of the Parmesan. Add ½ teaspoon freshly grated nutmeg for a more intense flavour.

rigatoni with aubergine & ricotta

Serves **4**
Preparation time **5 minutes**
Cooking time **35 minutes**

2 large **aubergines**
olive oil, for frying
2 **garlic cloves**, finely
   chopped
2 x 400 g (13 oz) cans
   chopped tomatoes
20 **basil leaves**, torn
400 g (13 oz) **dried rigatoni**
200 g (7 oz) **ricotta cheese**
3 tablespoons freshly grated
   pecorino cheese
salt and black pepper

Cut the aubergines into quarters lengthways, then each quarter in half lengthways. Cut the pieces into finger-sized lengths.

Heat 1 cm (½ inch) oil in a large frying pan over a high heat until the surface of the oil seems to shimmer. Add the aubergines, in batches, and fry until golden. With a slotted spoon, remove and drain on kitchen paper.

Heat 1 tablespoon oil in a large, heavy-based frying pan over a medium heat, add the garlic and cook, stirring, for 30 seconds. Stir in the aubergines and season, then stir in the tomatoes. Bring to the boil, then reduce the heat and simmer, uncovered, for 20 minutes until the sauce has thickened. Remove from the heat, stir in half the basil and adjust the seasoning.

When the sauce is almost ready, cook the pasta in a large saucepan of salted boiling water according to the packet instructions until al dente. Drain, reserving a ladleful of the cooking water. Add the pasta to the sauce and stir over a low heat. Pour in the reserved pasta cooking water and continue stirring until the pasta is well coated and looks silky. Serve immediately with a scattering of ricotta, pecorino and the remaining basil.

For rigatoni with pumpkin & ricotta, replace the aubergine with 500 g (1 lb) peeled, deseeded and diced pumpkin. Fry and drain on kitchen paper as above. Cook 2 thinly sliced red onions in olive oil for 10 minutes until softened. Add the pumpkin and cook for 6–8 minutes until caramelized. Remove from the heat, stir in half the basil and continue as above.

pasta with garlic, oil & chilli

Serves **4–6**
Preparation time **5 minutes**
Cooking time **8 minutes**

400–600 g (13 oz–1 lb 2 oz)
   dried spaghettini
125 ml (4 fl oz) **olive oil**
2 **garlic cloves**, finely
   chopped
2 small **dried red chillies**,
   deseeded and chopped
2 tablespoons chopped
   parsley
salt and black pepper

Cook the pasta in a large saucepan of salted boiling water according to the packet instructions until al dente.

Meanwhile, heat the oil in a saucepan over a low heat, add the garlic and a pinch of salt and cook, stirring constantly, until the garlic is golden. If the garlic becomes too brown, it will taste bitter. Stir in the chillies.

Drain the pasta and add to the saucepan with the warm but not sizzling garlic, oil and chillies. Add plenty of pepper and the parsley and toss to combine. Serve immediately.

For Roman garlic, oil & chilli pasta, keep it simple by omitting the black pepper and parsley from the recipe. This dish is also excellent topped with soft poached eggs. Allow 2 eggs per portion.

fettuccine all' alfredo

Serves **4**
Preparation time **5 minutes**
Cooking time **5–15 minutes**

400 g (13 oz) **dried
  fettuccine** or **tagliatelle** or
  homemade fettuccine or
  tagliatelle using 1 quantity
  3-egg Pasta Dough (see
  page 10)
50 g (2 oz) **unsalted butter**
200 ml (7 fl oz) **double cream**
large pinch of freshly grated
  nutmeg
50g (2 oz) **Parmesan cheese**,
  freshly grated, plus extra for
  serving
6 tablespoons **milk**
salt and black pepper

Cook the pasta in a large saucepan of salted boiling water until al dente. Cook according to the packet instructions for dried pasta or for 2 minutes if using fresh pasta.

Meanwhile, melt the butter in a wide, heavy-based pan. Add the cream and bring to the boil. Reduce the heat and simmer for 1 minute until slightly thickened.

Drain the pasta thoroughly, then toss it into the pan with the cream sauce over a very low heat. Add the nutmeg, Parmesan and milk, and season with salt and pepper. Toss gently until the sauce has thickened and the pasta is well coated. Serve immediately with a scattering of grated Parmesan.

For alfredo sauce with sun-dried tomatoes & asparagus, add 100 g (3½ oz) chopped sun-dried (semi-blush) tomatoes and 250 g (8 oz) blanched asparagus tips just before serving.

goats' cheese linguine with herbs

Serves **4**
Preparation time **5 minutes**
Cooking time **10–12 minutes**

250 g (8 oz) **dried linguine**
300 g (10 oz) **firm goats'
cheese**
1 **lemon**
75 g (3 oz) **butter**
2 tablespoons **olive oil**, plus
extra for oiling
3 **shallots**, finely chopped
2 **garlic cloves**, crushed
25 g (1 oz) **mixed chopped
herbs**, such as tarragon,
chervil, parsley and dill
3 tablespoons **capers** in brine,
rinsed and drained
salt and black pepper

Cook the pasta in a large saucepan of boiling salted water according to the packet instructions until al dente.

Meanwhile, thickly slice the goats' cheese and arrange on a lightly oiled, foil-lined grill rack. Cook under a preheated hot grill for 2 minutes, or until golden. Set aside and keep warm.

Using a zester, pare strips of rind from the lemon, then squeeze the juice.

Melt the butter with the oil in a frying pan or sauté pan over a medium heat. Add the shallots and garlic and cook gently, stirring, for 3 minutes. Stir in the herbs, capers and lemon juice. Season with salt and pepper.

Drain the pasta lightly, so that it retains plenty of moisture and does not dry out the sauce, and return to the pan. Add the goats' cheese and herb mixture and toss the ingredients together gently. Serve immediately with a scattering of the lemon rind strips.

For linguine with omelette & herbs, use 6 eggs in place of the goats' cheese. Beat 3 eggs with seasoning, heat a knob of butter in a frying pan, add the eggs and cook until set, lifting the edges of the omelette with a spatula to let the liquid run underneath. Turn out and repeat with the other 3 eggs. Roll up and finely slice the omelettes, adding the strips to the pasta with the sautéed shallots, garlic, herbs, capers and lemon juice.

ravioli with tomato & cream sauce

Serves **4**
Preparation time **10 minutes**
Cooking time **25 minutes**

15 g (½ oz) **unsalted butter**
1 tablespoon **olive oil**
½ **onion**, finely chopped
½ **celery stick**, finely chopped
350 ml (12 fl oz) **passata (sieved tomatoes)**
large pinch of **caster sugar**
250 g (8 oz) **fresh spinach and ricotta ravioli**
100 ml (3½ fl oz) **double cream**
large pinch of freshly grated **nutmeg**
salt and black pepper
fresh **Parmesan cheese shavings**, to serve
basil leaves, to garnish

Melt the butter with the oil in a heavy-based saucepan over a low heat. Add the onion and celery and cook, stirring occasionally, for 10 minutes until softened but not coloured. Stir in the passata and sugar and bring to the boil. Reduce the heat and gently simmer, uncovered, for 10 minutes until thickened. Season with salt and pepper.

Cook the ravioli in a large saucepan of salted boiling water according to the packet instructions until al dente. Meanwhile, add the cream to the sauce and bring to the boil. Stir in the nutmeg and remove from the heat.

Drain the pasta thoroughly and transfer to a serving dish. Spoon over the sauce and serve immediately with a scattering of Parmesan shavings and garnished with basil leaves.

For gnocchi with almonds, tomato & cream, replace the ravioli with 500 g (1 lb) gnocchi, cooked for 3–4 minutes or according to packet instructions in salted boiling water. Prepare the tomato sauce as above, scattering the sauce with 1 tablespoon toasted flaked almonds before serving.

rigatoni with courgettes & feta

Serves **4**
Preparation time **15 minutes**
Cooking time **10–12 minutes**

375 g (12 oz) **dried rigatoni**
3 **courgettes**, cut into 1 cm
 (½ inch) thick slices
6 tablespoons **olive oil**
2 **lemon thyme sprigs**
½ **lemon**, for squeezing
200 g (7 oz) **feta cheese**, cut
 into cubes
12 **green olives**, pitted and
 roughly chopped
salt and black pepper

Cook the pasta in a large saucepan of salted boiling water according to the packet instructions until al dente. Drain thoroughly.

Meanwhile, put the courgettes in a large bowl and toss with 1 tablespoon of the oil. Heat a ridged griddle pan over a high heat until smoking. Add the courgette slices and cook for 2–3 minutes on each side until lightly charred and tender.

Return the courgette slices to the bowl. Drizzle with the remaining oil, scatter over the lemon thyme sprigs and squeeze over the juice from the lemon half. Season with salt and pepper.

Drain the pasta thoroughly and add it to the bowl with the feta and olives. Toss well to combine and serve the pasta immediately.

For rigatoni with artichoke hearts & taleggio, use 2 x 400 g (13 oz) cans artichoke hearts instead of the courgettes. Drain and halve the artichoke hearts, toss with 1 tablespoon oil and stir-fry with 1 tablespoon finely chopped rosemary for 2 minutes. Omit the lemon juice. Combine with the green olives and 150 g (5 oz) taleggio, cut into cubes, and the cooked pasta.

dolcelatte & spinach gnocchi

Serves **4**
Preparation time **5 minutes**
Cooking time **20 minutes**

500 g (1 lb) **bought gnocchi**
 or **1 quantity Classic Potato**
 Gnocchi (see page 218)
15 g (½ oz) **unsalted butter**
125 g (4 oz) **baby spinach**
large pinch of freshly grated
 nutmeg
175 g (6 oz) **dolcelatte**
 cheese, cut into cubes
125 ml (4 fl oz) **double cream**
3 tablespoons freshly grated
 Parmesan cheese
salt and black pepper

Cook the gnocchi in a large saucepan of salted boiling water until they rise to the surface: according to the packet instructions for bought gnocchi or for 3–4 minutes if using homemade. Drain thoroughly.

Meanwhile, melt the butter in a saucepan over a high heat, and when it starts to sizzle, add the spinach and cook, stirring, for 1 minute, or until just wilted. Remove from the heat and season with nutmeg, salt and pepper, then stir in the dolcelatte, cream and gnocchi.

Transfer to an ovenproof dish and scatter with the Parmesan. Bake in a preheated oven, 220°C (425°F), Gas Mark 7, for 12–15 minutes until the sauce is bubbling and golden.

For dolcelatte, kale & leek gnocchi, replace the spinach with 250 g (8 oz) finely shredded kale and 1 finely sliced leek, cooked in butter for 3–4 minutes. Omit the nutmeg. Season with salt and pepper and combine with the dolcelatte, cream and gnocchi. Bake as above.

pesto trapanese

Serves **4**
Preparation time **10 minutes**
Cooking time **10–12 minutes**

400 g (13 oz) **dried spaghetti**
2 **garlic cloves**, peeled
50 g (2 oz) **basil leaves**, plus
    extra to garnish
2 **fresh red chillies**, deseeded
400 g (13 oz) **ripe tomatoes**,
    roughly chopped
150 g (5 oz) **almonds with
    skin on**, coarsely ground
150 ml (¼ pint) **extra virgin
    olive oil**
salt
freshly grated **pecorino
    cheese**, to serve (optional)

Cook the pasta in a large saucepan of salted boiling water according to the packet instructions until al dente.

Meanwhile, put the garlic cloves, basil, chillies and tomatoes in a food processor and process until finely chopped but not smooth. Stir in the ground almonds and oil, and season with salt.

Drain the pasta and return to the pan. Add the pesto and stir thoroughly. Serve immediately with a scattering of grated pecorino, if you like, and garnished with basil leaves.

For prawn & pesto trapanese salad, replace the spaghetti with 300 g (10 oz) small pasta shapes. Refresh the cooked pasta under cold running water before stirring in 250 g (8 oz) cooked prawns and the pesto.

puttanesca

Serves **4**
Preparation time **10 minutes**
Cooking time **20 minutes**

2 tablespoons **capers** in salt
  or brine
4 tablespoons **olive oil**
large pinch of **crushed dried
  chillies**
1 **garlic clove**, crushed
8 **anchovy fillets** in oil,
  drained and roughly
  chopped
400 g (13 oz) can **chopped
  tomatoes**
75 g (3 oz) **pitted black
  olives**, roughly chopped
400 g (13 oz) **dried spaghetti**
salt

Rinse the capers and, if you are using capers in salt, soak them in cold water for 5 minutes, then drain; if using capers in brine, simply rinse, then drain.

Meanwhile, heat the oil in a large frying pan over a low heat. Add the chillies, garlic and anchovies and cook, stirring, for 2 minutes until the anchovies begin to melt into the oil. Increase the heat to high, add the capers and cook, stirring, for 1 minute. Add the tomatoes and olives, season with salt and bring to the boil. Leave the sauce to boil rapidly while you cook the pasta.

Cook the pasta in a large saucepan of salted boiling water according to the packet instructions until al dente. Drain, reserving a ladleful of the cooking water. Stir the pasta into the sauce, tossing until well combined. Add the reserved pasta cooking water and continue stirring until the pasta is well coated and looks silky. Serve immediately.

For tuna puttanesca, add 200 g (7 oz) canned, drained tuna to the sauce, stirred into the frying pan together with the capers.

mascarpone & mixed herb pasta

Serves **4**
Preparation time **5 minutes**
Cooking time **10–20 minutes**

1 tablespoon **olive oil**
10 **sun-dried tomatoes** in oil,
   thinly sliced
2 **garlic cloves**, crushed
200 g (7 oz) **mascarpone
   cheese**
125 ml (4 fl oz) **milk**
4 tablespoons **mixed
   chopped herbs** (a
   combination of flat leaf
   parsley, basil, chives, thyme
   and/or chervil)
400 g (13 oz) **dried
   tagliatelle** or **fettuccine** or
   homemade tagliatelle or
   fettuccine using 1 quantity
   3-egg Pasta Dough (see
   page 10)
3 tablespoons freshly grated
   Parmesan cheese, plus
   extra to serve
salt and black pepper

Pour the oil into a large frying pan, add the tomatoes and garlic and place over a very low heat. Leave the flavours to infuse for 5 minutes. If the garlic begins to colour, simply remove the pan from the hob and leave to infuse in the heat of the pan. Add the mascarpone and milk and stir until the mascarpone has melted. Remove from the heat and stir the herbs through the sauce. Season with salt and pepper.

Cook the pasta in a large saucepan of salted boiling water until it is al dente: according to the packet instructions for dried pasta or for 2 minutes if using fresh pasta. Drain thoroughly, reserving a ladleful of the cooking water.

Return the frying pan with the sauce to a low heat and gently toss in the pasta and Parmesan until well coated. Add some of the reserved pasta cooking water to loosen the sauce to a silky consistency. Serve immediately with some grated Parmesan on the side.

For mascarpone, mixed nuts & herb pasta, add 50 g (2 oz) toasted hazelnuts and 3 tablespoons pine nuts to the sauce before adding the pasta.

wholewheat pasta with cabbage

Serves **4**

Preparation time **15 minutes**

Cooking time **25 minutes**

250 g (8 oz) **potatoes**, peeled and cut into 2.5 cm (1 inch) pieces

375 g (12 oz) **dried wholewheat pasta shapes** of your choice

300 g (10 oz) **Savoy cabbage**, shredded

1 tablespoon **olive oil**

2 **garlic cloves**, finely chopped

200 g (7 oz) **mascarpone cheese**

200 g (7 oz) **Gorgonzola cheese**, crumbled

salt and black pepper

freshly grated **Parmesan cheese**, to serve

Cook the potatoes in a large saucepan of salted boiling water for 5 minutes, then add the pasta and cook according to the packet instructions until al dente. When there are 5 minutes of the cooking time remaining, add the cabbage.

Meanwhile, heat the oil in a small saucepan over a low heat. Add the garlic and, as it starts to colour, tip in the mascarpone and Gorgonzola, stirring until melted. Remove from the heat.

Just before draining the pasta, stir a ladleful of the cooking water into the cheese sauce. Drain the pasta and transfer to a large serving bowl. Pour in the cheese sauce, toss well to combine and serve immediately with a scattering of grated Parmesan.

For wholewheat pasta with cranberries & red cabbage, omit the Savoy cabbage and instead stir-fry 250 g (8 oz) finely shredded red cabbage in oil with the garlic until the cabbage is tender but retains some bite. Melt the cheese in a separate pan, then combine with the cabbage, garlic and 4 tablespoons dried cranberries. Finish as above.

red pepper & pecorino pesto

Serves **4**

Preparation time **10 minutes**

Cooking time **25 minutes**

5 **red peppers**

1 tablespoon **extra virgin olive oil**, plus extra to serve

50 g (2 oz) **blanched almonds**

1 **garlic clove**, peeled

30 g (1¼ oz) **pecorino cheese**, freshly grated

400 g (13 oz) **dried penne**

65 g (2½ oz) **wild rocket**

salt and black pepper

Rub the peppers with the oil and cook under a preheated very hot grill, turning occasionally, until black and blistered all over. Transfer the peppers to a bowl, cover with clingfilm and leave to steam for 5 minutes. This will make it easier to peel off the skins.

When the peppers are cool enough to handle, peel off the skins. Cut one of the peppers into strips, trimming off the white core and seeds as you go, and reserve. Trim the remaining peppers.

Put the trimmed peppers in a food processor with the almonds, garlic clove and pecorino and process until smooth. Season with salt and pepper. Transfer to a serving bowl.

Cook the pasta in a large saucepan of salted boiling water according to the packet instructions until it is al dente. Drain the pasta and add it to the sauce with the reserved pepper strips and rocket. Toss through the pasta. Serve immediately with a generous drizzle of extra virgin olive oil.

For preserved pepper & smoked cheese pesto, use a 250 g (8 oz) bottle roasted peppers and 50 g (2 oz) smoked cheese, such as smoked manchego. Drain the bottled peppers and cut them into strips, and grate the cheese. Finely chop the other ingredients and combine them with the peppers and cheese. Stir in the pasta and rocket, then serve.

fettuccine with gorgonzola sauce

Serves **4**
Preparation time **5 minutes**
Cooking time **12–14 minutes**

500 g (1 lb) **dried fettuccine**
   or other **ribbon pasta**
25 g (1 oz) **butter**, plus extra
   to serve
250 g (8 oz) **Gorgonzola**
   cheese, crumbled
150 ml (¼ pint) **double cream**
2 tablespoons **dry vermouth**
1 teaspoon **cornflour**
2 tablespoons chopped **sage**
   leaves, plus extra leaves to
   garnish
salt and black pepper

Cook the pasta in a large saucepan of salted boiling water according to the packet instructions until al dente.

Meanwhile, melt the butter in a heavy-based saucepan over a very low heat. Add the Gorgonzola and heat, stirring, for 2–3 minutes until the cheese has melted.

Add the cream, vermouth and cornflour and whisk well to combine. Stir in the sage. Cook, whisking constantly, until the sauce boils and thickens. Season with salt and pepper and remove from the heat.

Drain the pasta thoroughly and toss with a little butter. Reheat the sauce gently, whisking well. Pour over the pasta and toss well to combine. Serve immediately, garnished with sage leaves.

For beetroot & raspberry vinegar salad, to serve as a side dish, dice 250 g (8 oz) peeled, cooked beetroot and toss with ½ finely chopped small onion. Mix together 1 teaspoon caster sugar, 2–3 tablespoons raspberry vinegar and 2 tablespoons olive or walnut oil, and drizzle over the salad.

aubergine & rigatoni bake

Serves **4–6**
Preparation time **30 minutes**, plus standing
Cooking time **40 minutes**

olive oil, for frying
3 large **aubergines**, cut into 5 mm (¼ inch) slices
1½ tablespoons **dried oregano**
375 g (12 oz) **dried penne** or **rigatoni**
1 quantity **Quickest-ever Tomato Pasta Sauce** (see page 136)
2 x 150 g (5 oz) **mozzarella balls**, roughly chopped
75 g (3 oz) **Parmesan cheese**, freshly grated
2 tablespoons **fresh white breadcrumbs**
salt and black pepper

Heat 1 cm (½ inch) oil in a large frying pan over a high heat until the surface of the oil seems to shimmer slightly. Add the aubergines, in batches, and fry until golden on both sides. Remove with a slotted spoon and drain on a dish lined with kitchen paper. Scatter with the oregano and season lightly with salt.

Cook the pasta in a large saucepan of salted boiling water according to the packet instructions until almost al dente. Drain, then stir in a bowl with the tomato sauce, mozzarella and Parmesan. Season with salt and pepper.

Meanwhile, line the base and sides of an 18 cm (7 inch) springform cake tin with the aubergine slices. Overlap the slices slightly, to ensure that there are no gaps, then fill the tin with the pasta mixture. Press down so that the pasta is tightly packed, then cover with the remaining aubergine slices.

Scatter the breadcrumbs over the top of the pasta cake and bake on a baking sheet in a preheated oven, 200°C (400°F), Gas Mark 6, for 15 minutes until golden brown. Leave the cake to stand for 15 minutes before unclipping and removing the ring to serve. Don't attempt to remove the cake from its base, as it will most probably break in the process.

For courgette & rigatoni bake, use 6–7 large courgettes instead of the aubergines and cut them into long slices before frying.

mushroom & mozzarella lasagne

Serves **4**
Preparation time **20 minutes**
Cooking time **20 minutes**

8 **dried lasagne sheets**
50 g (2 oz) **butter**
2 tablespoons **olive oil**, plus
  extra for oiling
2 **onions**, chopped
2 **garlic cloves**, crushed
500 g (1 lb) **mushrooms**,
  sliced
4 tablespoons **double cream**
4 tablespoons **dry white wine**
1 teaspoon chopped **thyme**
2 **red peppers**, roasted, then
  skinned, cored, deseeded
  and thickly sliced (see
  page 186)
125 g (4 oz) **baby spinach**,
  chopped
125 g (4 oz) **buffalo**
  mozzarella cheese, sliced
50 g (2 oz) **Parmesan**
  cheese, freshly shaved
salt and black pepper

Cook the pasta sheets, in batches, in a large saucepan of salted boiling water according to the packet instructions until they are just al dente. Drain, refresh in cold water and lay on a tea towel to drain thoroughly. Place 4 sheets in the base of a well-oiled, large ovenproof dish.

Meanwhile, melt the butter with the oil in a saucepan over a medium heat. Add the onions and cook, stirring, for 3 minutes. Add the garlic and cook, stirring, for 1 minute. Add the mushrooms, increase the heat to high and cook, stirring frequently, for 5 minutes. Add the cream, wine and thyme, and season with salt and pepper. Simmer for 4 minutes.

Place a generous spoonful of the mushroom mixture on each pasta sheet and add some red pepper slices and half the spinach. Top with the remaining pasta sheets. Add the remaining spinach, a slice of mozzarella and top with a little more mushroom mixture. Finish with some Parmesan shavings.

Place under a preheated very hot grill and cook for 5 minutes, or until the mushroom mixture is bubbling and the Parmesan is golden. Serve immediately.

For rich mushroom & fontina lasagna, replace the mozzarella with 125 g (4 oz) fontina and use a mixture of 250 g (8 oz) chestnut mushrooms and 250 g (8 oz) shitake mushrooms.

pasta with fresh tomato & basil

Serves **4**
Preparation time **10 minutes**
Cooking time **17–20 minutes**

3 tablespoons **olive oil**
2 **garlic cloves**, finely
   chopped
1 kg (2 lb) **very ripe plum**
   tomatoes, skinned and
   chopped
2 teaspoons **good-quality**
   aged balsamic vinegar
about 30 **basil leaves**
400 g (13 oz) **dried pasta** of
   your choice
salt and black pepper
freshly grated **Parmesan**
   cheese or **extra virgin olive**
   oil, to serve

Heat the oil in a large frying pan over a high heat, add the garlic and cook, stirring, for 30 seconds. Quickly stir in the tomatoes. Bring to the boil, season with salt and pepper and cook for 6–7 minutes, squashing the tomatoes down slightly to release their juice.

Remove from the heat and stir in the vinegar and basil. Leave the flavour of the basil to infuse into the sauce while you cook the pasta.

Cook the pasta in a large saucepan of salted boiling water according to the packet instructions until al dente. Transfer the sauce to a serving bowl. Drain the pasta thoroughly, then stir into the sauce. Serve immediately with a drizzle of extra virgin olive oil or a scattering of grated Parmesan.

For pasta-stuffed peppers, halve and deseed 4 large peppers and grill them cut side down until the skins have blackened. Allow to cool, then peel. Make the tomato sauce as above and combine with 250 g (8 oz) small pasta shapes, cooked, drained, rinsed and drained again. Place the peppers in a large shallow dish and fill each pepper with a quarter of the pasta mixture. Top with 150 g (5 oz) sliced mozzarella and cook under a preheated medium grill until the cheese is bubbling and golden.

rigatoni with pumpkin & ricotta

Serves **4**
Preparation time **10 minutes**
Cooking time **18–23 minutes**

25 g (1 oz) **unsalted butter**
1 small **onion**, finely chopped
20 **sage leaves**
250 g (8 oz) **pumpkin** or
   butternut squash, peeled
   and deseeded
400 g (13 oz) **dried rigatoni**
50 g (2 oz) **Parmesan
   cheese**, freshly grated
200 g (7 oz) **ricotta cheese**
25g (1 oz) **flaked almonds**,
   toasted
salt and black pepper

Melt the butter in a large, heavy-based saucepan over a low heat. Add the onion and sage and cook, stirring occasionally, for 6–8 minutes until the onion is softened.

Cut the pumpkin or squash into 1 cm (½ inch) pieces, add to the pan and season with salt and pepper. Cook for 12–15 minutes until the pumpkin is very tender.

Meanwhile, cook the pasta in a large saucepan of salted boiling water according to the packet instructions until al dente. Drain.

Toss the pasta in the sauce with the Parmesan and the ricotta. Serve the pasta immediately, scattered with the flaked almonds.

For rigatoni with pumpkin, ricotta & amaretti, with a lovely crunchy finish, use 25 g (1 oz) crumbled amaretti biscuits instead of the almonds.

tomato, pine nut & rocket pesto

Serves **4–6**
Preparation time **10 minutes**
Cooking time **10–12 minutes**

400–600 g (13–1 lb 2 oz)
dried pasta twists, such
as fusilli
3 **ripe tomatoes**
4 **garlic cloves**, peeled
50 g (2 oz) **rocket leaves**,
plus extra to garnish
100 g (3½ oz) **pine nuts**
150 ml (¼ pint) **olive oil**
salt and black pepper

Cook the pasta in a large saucepan of salted boiling water according to the packet instructions until al dente.

Meanwhile, finely chop the tomatoes, garlic cloves, rocket and pine nuts by hand, then stir in the oil. Season with salt and pepper. Transfer to a bowl.

Drain the pasta, add to the bowl with the pesto and toss to combine. Serve immediately, garnished with a few basil leaves.

For tomato, parsley & almond pesto, put 4 ripe tomatoes, 2 cloves garlic, 50 g (2 oz) parsley, 100 g (3½ oz) almonds and 150 ml (½ pint) olive oil in a food processor and process until smooth.

ricotta-baked large pasta shells

Serves **4**
Preparation time **20 minutes**
Cooking time **30 minutes**

250 g (8 oz) **dried conchiglie rigate**
400 g (13 oz) **ricotta cheese**
1 small **garlic clove**, crushed
125 g (4 oz) **Parmesan cheese**, freshly grated
20 g (¾ oz) **basil**, finely chopped
125 g (4 oz) **baby spinach**, roughly chopped
1 quantity **Quickest-ever Tomato Pasta Sauce** (see page 136)
150 g (5 oz) **mozzarella cheese**, cut into cubes
salt and black pepper

Cook the pasta in a large saucepan of salted boiling water according to the packet instructions until al dente. Drain, refresh in cold water, then drain again thoroughly.

Meanwhile, make the filling. Put the ricotta in a large bowl and break up with a fork. Stir in the garlic, half the Parmesan, the basil and spinach. Season generously with salt and pepper and use this mixture to stuff the pasta shells.

Spoon one quarter of the tomato sauce over the base of an ovenproof dish and arrange the pasta shells, open-side uppermost, on top. Pour the remaining sauce evenly over, then scatter with the mozzarella and the remaining Parmesan.

Bake in a preheated oven, 220°C (425°F), Gas Mark 7, for 20 minutes until golden brown.

For watercress & chickpea shells with béchamel, use 1 quantity béchamel sauce from the Spring Cannelloni recipe (see page 202) instead of the tomato sauce. Finely chop 150 g (5 oz) watercress and combine with 2 chopped spring onions and a 400 g (13 oz) can chickpeas, drained and chopped. Mix with the ricotta, parmesan and basil as above, omitting the garlic and spinach. Layer the béchamel and filled pasta shells, then top with cheese as above.

spring cannelloni

Serves **4**
Preparation time **30 minutes**
Cooking time **30–40 minutes**

500 ml (17 fl oz) **milk**
1 **bay leaf**
1 small **onion**, quartered
125 g (4 oz) shelled **broad beans**, fresh or frozen
125 g (4 oz) shelled **peas**, fresh or frozen
20 g (¾ oz) **mint**, chopped
20 g (¾ oz) **basil**, chopped
1 **garlic clove**, crushed
300 g (10 oz) **ricotta cheese**
75 g (3 oz) **Parmesan cheese**, plus extra for sprinkling
40 g (1½ oz) **butter**
30 g (1¼ oz) **plain flour**
75 ml (3 fl oz) **dry white wine**
150 g (5 oz) **dried lasagne sheets**
salt and black pepper

Bring the milk with the bay leaf and onion to a simmer in a saucepan. Infuse off the heat for 20 minutes. Strain.

Meanwhile, cook the beans and peas in boiling water until tender: 6–8 minutes for fresh or 2 minutes for frozen. Drain and refresh in cold water. Process half in a food processor with the herbs and garlic to a rough purée. Combine with the ricotta, Parmesan and remaining vegetables. Season with salt and pepper.

Melt the butter in a saucepan over a very low heat. Add the flour and cook, stirring, for 2 minutes until a light biscuit colour. Remove from the heat and slowly add the infused milk, stirring away any lumps as you go. Return to the heat, bring to a simmer, stirring, and pour in the wine. Simmer for 5–6 minutes until thick. Season with salt and pepper.

Cook the pasta in a large saucepan of salted boiling water according to the packet instructions until just al dente. Drain, refresh in cold water, then cut into 16 pieces 8 x 9 cm (3¼ x 3½ inches).

Spread 1½ tablespoons of filling on to each pasta piece and roll up. Spread half the sauce in an ovenproof dish and top with the rolls in a single layer. Spoon over the remaining sauce. Sprinkle with Parmesan. Bake in a preheated oven, 200°C (400°F), Gas Mark 6, for 15 minutes until golden brown.

For spinach cannelloni, chop and wilt 250 g (8 oz) spinach in a little butter in a covered pan and use instead of the beans and peas. Cook as above, replacing the mint and basil with grated nutmeg.

vegetable spaghetti bolognese

Serves **2**
Preparation time **15 minutes**
Cooking time **35–45 minutes**

1 tablespoon **vegetable oil**
1 **onion**, finely chopped
1 **garlic clove**, finely chopped
1 **celery stick**, finely chopped
1 **carrot**, finely chopped
75 g (3 oz) **chestnut mushrooms**, roughly chopped
1 tablespoon **tomato purée**
400 g (13 oz) can **chopped tomatoes**
250 ml (8 fl oz) **red wine** or **vegetable stock**
pinch of **dried mixed herbs**
1 teaspoon **yeast extract**
150 g (5 oz) **textured vegetable protein** (TVP)
2 tablespoons chopped **parsley**
200 g (7 oz) **wholewheat spaghetti**
salt and black pepper
freshly grated **Parmesan cheese**, to serve

Heat the oil in a large, heavy-based saucepan over a medium heat. Add the onion, garlic, celery, carrot and mushrooms and cook, stirring frequently for 5 minutes, or until softened. Add the tomato purée and cook, stirring, for a further minute.

Add the tomatoes, wine or stock, herbs, yeast extract and TVP. Bring to the boil, then reduce the heat, cover and simmer for 30–40 minutes until the TVP is tender. Stir in the parsley and season with salt and pepper.

Meanwhile, cook the pasta in a large pan of salted boiling water according to the packet instructions until it is al dente. Drain thoroughly, then divide the pasta between 2 serving plates. Top with the vegetable mixture and serve immediately with a scattering of grated Parmesan.

For lentil bolognaise, use 150 g (5 oz) canned green lentils in place of the TVP. Rinse them well before use. If you are using dried lentils, soak and cook them first according to the packet instructions.

garganelli with creamy cavolo nero

Serves **4**
Preparation time **10 minutes**
Cooking time **16–18 minutes**

500 g (1 lb) **cavolo nero
  (Italian black cabbage)**
3 tablespoons **olive oil**
2 **garlic cloves**, thinly sliced
1 **dried red chilli**, finely
  chopped
400 g (13 oz) **dried
  garganelli** or **fusilli**
300 ml (½ pint) **double cream**
50 g (2 oz) **pecorino cheese**,
  freshly grated, plus extra
  to serve
salt

Trim the cavolo nero, removing the tough central stalks, then roughly shred.

Heat the oil in a large frying pan over a medium heat, add the garlic and chilli and cook, stirring, until the garlic just begins to colour. Toss in the cavolo nero and season with salt. Cook, stirring, over a high heat for 2–3 minutes until softened.

Cook the pasta in a large saucepan of salted boiling water according to the packet instructions until al dente. Drain, reserving a ladleful of the cooking water.

Meanwhile, pour the cream over the wilted cabbage and bring to the boil. Reduce the heat to a slow simmer and cook for 5 minutes until the cream has thickened so that it coats the cabbage in a silky sauce. Add the pecorino and pasta and stir over a low heat for 30 seconds. Pour in the reserved pasta cooking water and continue stirring until the pasta is well coated and looks silky. Serve immediately with a scattering of grated pecorino.

For garganelli with cavolo nero & borlotti beans, drain a 400 g (13 oz) can borlotti beans and add to the cooked cavolo nero and onion and garlic mixture. Stir in a pinch of ground mace and the grated rind of 1 lemon, then add the cream and continue as above.

pasta primavera

Serves **4**

Preparation time **15 minutes**

Cooking time **10–12 minutes**

300 g (10 oz) **dried tagliatelle**

2 tablespoons **olive oil**

1 **garlic clove**, crushed

2 **shallots**, chopped

125 g (4 oz) shelled **fresh peas**

125 g (4 oz) **fresh young broad beans**, shelled

125 g (4 oz) **asparagus**, trimmed

125 g (4 oz) **spinach**, chopped

150 ml (¼ pint) **whipping cream**

75 g (3 oz) **Parmesan cheese**, freshly grated

handful of **mint leaves**, chopped

salt and black pepper

Cook the pasta in a large saucepan of salted boiling water according to the packet instructions until al dente.

Meanwhile, heat the oil in a saucepan over a medium heat, add the garlic and shallots and cook, stirring, for 3 minutes. Add the peas, beans, asparagus and spinach and cook, stirring, for 2 minutes. Stir the cream into the vegetables and simmer for 3 minutes.

Drain the pasta thoroughly, then add to the vegetable mixture and season well with salt and pepper. Add the Parmesan and mint and toss thoroughly with 2 spoons. Serve immediately

For pasta with tarragon-dressed vegetables, use 150 g (5 oz) each baby carrots, sugar snap peas and fine green beans and omit the spinach, peas and broad beans. Quarter the carrots and sugar snaps lengthways and blanch the green beans in boiling water, before cooking as above. Use a handful of tarragon leaves instead of mint.

spaghetti & courgette frittata

Serves **4**
Preparation time **10 minutes**
Cooking time **25 minutes**

2 tablespoons **olive oil**
1 **onion**, thinly sliced
2 **courgettes**, thinly sliced
1 **garlic clove**, crushed
4 **eggs**
125 g (4 oz) **cooked spaghetti**
4 tablespoons freshly grated **Parmesan cheese**
10 **basil leaves**, torn
salt and black pepper

Heat the oil in a heavy-based, ovenproof, nonstick 23 cm (9 inch) frying pan over a low heat. Add the onion and cook, stirring occasionally, for 6–8 minutes until softened. Stir in the courgettes and garlic and cook, stirring, for 2 minutes.

Beat the eggs in a large bowl and season with salt and pepper. Stir in the cooked vegetables, spaghetti and half the Parmesan and basil. Pour the mixture into the frying pan and quickly arrange the ingredients so they are evenly dispersed. Cook over a low heat for 8–10 minutes, or until all but the top of the frittata is set.

Transfer to a preheated very hot grill and place about 10 cm (4 inches) from the heat source. Cook until set but not coloured.

Give the pan a shake to loosen the frittata, then transfer to a plate. Scatter the top with the remaining Parmesan and basil and leave to cool for 5 minutes before serving.

For mixed vegetable frittata, use 300 g (10 oz) cooked spinach, peas and chopped broccoli in place of the courgettes, cooking as described above. Serve the frittata with a green salad.

mushroom & spinach lasagne

Serves **4**
Preparation time **15 minutes**
Cooking time **12 minutes**

3 tablespoons **extra virgin
olive oil**, plus extra for oiling
500 g (1 lb) **mixed
mushrooms**, sliced
200 g (7 oz) **mascarpone
cheese**
12 **bought fresh lasagne
sheets**
150 g (5 oz) **taleggio cheese**,
derinded and cut into cubes
125 g (4 oz) **baby spinach**
salt and black pepper

Heat the oil in a large frying pan over a medium heat, add the mushrooms and cook, stirring frequently, for 5 minutes. Add the mascarpone and cook over a high heat for 1 minute until thickened. Season with salt and pepper.

Meanwhile, put the pasta sheets in a large roasting tray and cover with boiling water. Leave to stand for 5 minutes, or until tender. Drain off the water.

Lightly oil an ovenproof dish and place 3 pasta sheets over the base, slightly overlapping. Top the pasta with a little of the taleggio, one-third of the mushroom sauce and one-third of the spinach. Repeat the process with 2 more layers then top the final layer of pasta with the remaining taleggio.

Place the lasagne under a preheated hot grill and cook for 5 minutes until the cheese is golden brown. Serve immediately.

For mushroom, tomato & courgette lasagna, use 500 g (1 lb) tomatoes and 2 courgettes in place of the spinach. Blanch the tomatoes in boiling water before peeling and slicing, and thinly slice the courgettes, before proceeding as above.

spaghetti with thai flavours

Serves **2**
Preparation time **10 minutes**
Cooking time **11–13 minutes**

200 g (7 oz) **dried spaghetti**
3 tablespoons **vegetable oil**
2 teaspoons **sesame oil**
2 **garlic cloves**, sliced
1 teaspoon grated **fresh root ginger**
2 **fresh red bird's eye chillies**, deseeded and finely chopped
finely grated **rind and juice of 2 limes**
1 bunch of **fresh coriander**, chopped
handful of **Thai** or **ordinary basil leaves**
salt and black pepper

Cook the pasta in a large saucepan of salted boiling water according to the packet instructions until al dente. Drain, reserving 4 tablespoons of the cooking water, and return the pasta to the pan.

Meanwhile, heat the 2 oils together in a frying pan over a medium heat, add the garlic, ginger, chillies and lime rind and cook, stirring, for 30 seconds, or until the garlic starts to release its aroma. Whisk in the reserved pasta cooking water and bring to the boil.

Stir into the pasta with the herbs and lime juice, and toss over the heat for a few seconds until heated through. Season with salt and pepper and serve immediately.

For seafood spaghetti with Thai flavours, add 200 g (7 oz) raw large peeled prawns to the hot oils and cook, stirring, for 2 minutes until they turn pink, before adding the garlic and other ingredients.

homemade

classic potato gnocchi

Serves **4–6**
Preparation time **30 minutes**,
  plus resting
Cooking time **30 minutes**

1 kg (2 lb) **floury potatoes**,
  such as King Edwards or
  Maris Piper
¼ **nutmeg**, freshly grated
150–300 g (5–10 oz) **plain
  flour**, plus extra for dusting
2 **eggs**
salt and black pepper

Put the unpeeled potatoes in a saucepan and cover with cold water. Cover with a lid and bring to the boil. Reduce the heat and simmer for 20 minutes, or until cooked through. Drain.

Peel the potatoes while still warm and pass them through a mouli or ricer to make a light, smooth mash. Put in a large bowl, add the nutmeg and season. Sift in 150 g (5 oz) flour, crack in the eggs and gently but quickly work the mixture through your fingers until it reaches a lumpy breadcrumb consistency.

Knead gently on a clean work surface to make a soft, smooth, pliable dough. Add more flour if the mixture is too wet. Be careful not to overwork the dough or the gnocchi will lose their light quality.

Divide the dough into 3 pieces and roll each piece into finger-thick lengths. Cut into 2.5 cm (1 inch) pieces with a sharp knife. Transfer to a floured baking sheet and leave to rest for 10–20 minutes.

Bring a large saucepan of salted water to the boil. Add the gnocchi and cook for 3–4 minutes, or until they rise to the surface. Remove with a slotted spoon and drain. Serve immediately with your sauce of choice.

For rocket or spinach gnocchi, add 50 g (2 oz) finely chopped wild rocket or baby spinach to the mixture before you knead it together.

rocket, potato & lemon ravioli

Serves **4**

Preparation time **25 minutes**

Cooking time **1 hour
5 minutes**

500 g (1 lb) **floury potatoes**,
such as King Edwards or
Maris Piper

3 tablespoons freshly grated
Parmesan cheese

75 g (3 oz) **wild rocket**, plus
extra to serve

finely grated **rind of 1
unwaxed lemon**

125 g (4 oz) **butter**

large pinch of freshly grated
nutmeg

1 quantity **3-egg Pasta
Dough** (see page 10)

Italian 00 or **fine plain flour**,
for dusting

salt and black pepper

fresh **Parmesan cheese
shavings**, to serve

Prick the potatoes all over with a fork and put on a large baking sheet. Bake in a preheated oven, 220°C (425°F), Gas Mark 7, for 1 hour, or until cooked through – to test, pierce the largest potato with a blunt knife.

When cool enough to handle, halve the potatoes and scoop the flesh out into a bowl. Mash in the Parmesan, rocket, lemon rind and half the butter. Add the nutmeg and season with salt and pepper.

Roll the pasta dough out into long sheets (see page 11). Working on one sheet at a time, add a heaped teaspoonful of filling every 5 cm (2 inches) until half the sheet is filled. Lightly brush with water and fold the empty side over the filling. Gently but firmly push down between the filling, sealing the pasta and ensuring there is no trapped air. Cut into squares or rounds using a pastry wheel, crinkle cutter or biscuit cutter. Transfer to a floured baking sheet and cover with a tea towel.

Cook the pasta in a large saucepan of salted boiling water for 2–3 minutes until al dente. Drain, reserving a ladleful of the cooking water.

Meanwhile, melt the remaining butter in a large frying pan over a low heat. Add the ravioli and its reserved cooking water and simmer gently until coated in a silky sauce. Serve immediately with a scattering of Parmesan shavings and rocket.

For watercress & mustard ravioli, try replacing the lemon rind and rocket with 2 teaspoons mustard and a handful of finely chopped parsley, 2 crushed garlic cloves and 75 g (3 oz) watercress.

duck tortellini

Serves **4**

Preparation time **40 minutes**

Cooking time **1½ hours**

25g (1 oz) **unsalted butter**

1 tablespoon **olive oil**

1 small **onion**, finely chopped

2 **celery sticks**, finely chopped

1 **carrot**, finely chopped

200 ml (7 fl oz) **dry white wine**

finely grated **rind and juice of 1 orange**

2 tablespoons chopped **thyme**

250 ml (8 fl oz) **canned chopped tomatoes**

2 skinless **duck legs**, about 175–200 g (6–7 oz) each

2 tablespoons freshly grated **Parmesan cheese**, plus extra to serve

2 tablespoons **fresh white breadcrumbs**

1 **egg**

1 quantity **3-egg Pasta Dough** (see page 10)

Italian 00 or **fine plain flour**, for dusting

salt and black pepper

chopped **flat leaf parsley**, to serve

Melt the butter with the oil in a large, heavy-based saucepan over a low heat. Add the onion, celery and carrot and cook for 10 minutes. Add the wine and boil for 1 minute. Add the orange rind and juice, thyme and tomatoes. Return to the boil.

Season the duck with salt and pepper. Add to the sauce and simmer gently, covered, for 1¼ hours until the meat flakes off the bone. Remove, then shred the flesh off the bone. Process in a food processor until finely chopped. Mix with the Parmesan, breadcrumbs and egg.

Roll the pasta dough out into long sheets (see page 11). Cut into 8 cm (3¼ inch) squares. Place a small ball of filling in the centre of each. Brush the edges with water, then fold the dough over the filling to make triangles. Gently but firmly push down between the filling to seal, ensuring that there is no trapped air. Bring the corners on the longest edge together and pinch tightly. Transfer to a floured baking sheet and cover with a tea towel.

Cook in a large saucepan of salted boiling water for 3–4 minutes until al dente. Meanwhile, reheat the sauce. Drain the pasta. Serve immediately with the sauce and a scattering of grated Parmesan and parsley.

For lamb or chicken tortellini, use 1 lamb shank or 2 chicken legs instead of the duck. Use orange rind and juice with lamb, but replace with lemon rind and juice for chicken. For a more intense flavour, use 200 ml (7 fl oz) red wine instead of the white wine.

ricotta & parma ham rotolo

Serves **4**
Preparation time **20 minutes**
Cooking time **35 minutes**

250 g (8 oz) **baby spinach**
250 g (8 oz) **ricotta cheese**
large pinch of freshly grated
 nutmeg
50 g (2 oz) **Parmesan
 cheese**, freshly grated, plus
 extra to serve
1 quantity **1-egg Pasta
 Dough** (see page 10)
3 slices of **Parma ham**
75 g (3 oz) **butter**, melted
salt and black pepper

Steam or microwave the spinach until just wilted. Refresh in cold water. Drain and squeeze out any liquid. Combine the ricotta, nutmeg and Parmesan. Season with salt and pepper.

Divide the pasta dough in half. Roll out each half into a sheet (see page 11). Lay a damp tea towel on a work surface and put the pasta sheets on top, overlapping them slightly to make a rectangle that covers most of the cloth. Brush a little water where the pasta sheets overlap and press firmly to seal.

Spread the ricotta mixture on to the pasta, leaving a 1.5 cm (¾ inch) border on the right and left. Scatter evenly with the spinach, then lay the Parma ham slices lengthways along the long edge nearest to you.

Brush the edges with water, then roll up the pasta, lifting the tea towel to help you. Pinch the edges to seal, then wrap in the tea towel. Tie both ends firmly with string and in 2–3 places along the length.

Cook the roll for 30 minutes in a fish kettle or deep baking dish of salted simmering water, using the kettle rack or a heatproof plate to keep the roll submerged.

Unwrap the roll, cut into 12 slices and arrange on individual plates. Drizzle with the melted butter and serve with a scattering of grated Parmesan.

For ricotta, watercress & speck rotolo, use 100 g (3½ oz) shredded speck and 250 g (8 oz) watercress instead of the spinach.

herb & wild mushroom ravioli

Serves **4**
Preparation time **35 minutes**
Cooking time **10–11 minutes**

2 tablespoons **olive oil**
2 **shallots**, finely chopped
250 g (8 oz) **mixed wild
    mushrooms**, finely chopped
25 g (1 oz) **Greek-style
    black olives**, pitted and
    finely chopped
4 **sun-dried tomato halves** in
    oil, drained and chopped
1 tablespoon **dry Marsala**
freshly grated **nutmeg**
1 quantity **2-egg Pasta
    Dough** (see page 10),
    with 4 tablespoons mixed
    chopped tarragon, marjoram
    and parsley
Italian 00 or **fine plain flour**,
    for dusting
50 g (2 oz) **butter**, melted
salt and black pepper
herb sprigs, to garnish

To serve
fresh **Parmesan shavings**
sautéed wild mushrooms

Heat the oil in a frying pan over a medium heat, add the shallots and cook, stirring frequently, for 5 minutes, or until soft and golden. Add the mushrooms, olives and tomatoes and cook over a high heat, stirring, for 2 minutes. Sprinkle with the Marsala and cook for a further minute. Season well with salt, pepper and nutmeg. Transfer to a bowl and leave to cool.

Roll the pasta dough out into long sheets (see page 11). Working on one sheet at a time, add a heaped teaspoonful of filling every 3.5 cm (1½ inches) until half the sheet is filled. Lightly brush with water and fold the empty side over the filling. Gently but firmly push down between the filling, sealing the pasta and ensuring that there is no trapped air. Cut into squares using a pastry wheel, crinkle cutter or a sharp knife. Transfer to a floured baking sheet and cover with a tea towel.

Cook the pasta in a large pan of salted boiling water for 2–3 minutes until al dente. Drain thoroughly, return to the pan and toss with the melted butter. Divide between 4 warmed serving plates and serve at once with a scattering of Parmesan shavings and sautéed wild mushrooms, garnished with herb sprigs.

For chestnut mushroom & walnut ravioli, use 250 g (8 oz) chestnut mushrooms and 100 g (3½ oz) walnuts instead of the wild mushrooms.

open seafood lasagne

Serves **4**
Preparation time **30 minutes**
Cooking time **35 minutes**

2 tablespoons **extra virgin
    olive oil**, plus extra for
    drizzling
1 small **onion**, finely chopped
1 **fennel bulb**, trimmed and
    finely chopped
2 **garlic cloves**, crushed
200 ml (7 fl oz) **dry white wine**
250 ml (7 fl oz) **canned
    chopped tomatoes**
1 quantity **1-egg Pasta
    Dough** (see page 10)
Italian 00 or **fine plain flour**,
    for dusting
handful of **flat leaf parsley
    leaves**
250 g (8 oz) **chunky white
    fish fillets**, such as cod,
    halibut or monkfish
250 g (8 oz) **delicate white
    fish fillets**, such as red
    mullet, red snapper, sea
    bass or sea bream
12 **raw peeled king prawns**
6 **basil leaves**, torn, plus extra
    to garnish
salt and black pepper

Heat the oil in a large, heavy-based saucepan over
a low heat. Add the onion and fennel and cook for
8–10 minutes until softened. Add the garlic and cook,
stirring, for 1 minute. Add the wine and boil rapidly
for 1 minute. Add the tomatoes and season with salt
and pepper. Bring to the boil, then simmer gently for
20 minutes.

Meanwhile, roll the pasta dough out into long sheets
(see page 11). Scatter half the length of each sheet
with parsley, then fold over to cover. Run through the
thinnest setting of the pasta machine, then cut into
12 rectangles. Lay on a floured tray, adding a dusting
of flour between any that overlap.

Cut the fish fillets into 3.5 cm (1½ inch) pieces. Add
the chunky fish to the sauce and simmer gently for
1 minute. Add the delicate fish and prawns and simmer
gently for 1 minute. Remove from the heat, stir in the
basil and cover.

Cook the pasta sheets, in batches, in a large saucepan
of boiling salted water for 2–3 minutes until al dente.
Drain, drizzle with oil and garnish with basil leaves.

Place a pasta sheet on each plate and top with half
the sauce. Repeat, finishing with a pasta sheet. Serve
immediately with a drizzle of oil.

saffron taglierini

Serves **4**
Preparation time **30 minutes**,
  plus chilling and soaking
Cooking time **12 minutes**

75 g (3 oz) **butter**
1 **onion**, finely chopped
100 ml (3½ fl oz) **vodka** or
  dry white wine
50 g (2 oz) **Parmesan
  cheese**, freshly grated

Pasta dough
0.4 g packet **saffron threads**
2 tablespoons **warm water**
225 g (7½ oz) **Italian 00** or
  fine plain flour, plus extra
  for dusting
75 g (3 oz) **semola di grano
  duro,** plus extra for dusting
2 **eggs,** plus 1 **egg yolk**

Soak the saffron threads in the measurement water for 15 minutes.

Use the pasta dough ingredients to prepare the dough following the method on page 10, adding the saffron threads and soaking water to the well in the flour after the eggs and egg yolk, or to the food processor with the other ingredients. Knead and chill as directed.

Roll the pasta dough out into long sheets (see page 11). Cut the pasta sheets into 20 cm (8 inch) lengths. Run the lengths through the finest cutters on the pasta machine's attachment to make taglierini. Place on a baking sheet dusted with semola and cover with a damp tea towel, for up to 3 hours.

Melt the butter in a large frying pan over a low heat, add the onion and cook, stirring occasionally, for 7–8 minutes until the onion is soft and translucent. Increase the heat to high and add the vodka or wine. Boil rapidly for 2 minutes, then remove from the heat.

Cook the pasta in a large saucepan of salted boiling water for 2–3 minutes until al dente. Drain and stir into the butter sauce. Serve immediately with the grated Parmesan.

For tarragon & lemon taglierini, use 2 tablespoons chopped tarragon and the finely grated zest of 1 lemon. Add to the well in the flour after the eggs, or to the food processor with the other ingredients, in place of the saffron.

spinach & ricotta ravioli

Serves **4**
Preparation time **25 minutes**
Cooking time **2–3 minutes**

500 g (1 lb) **frozen spinach**,
   defrosted and squeezed dry
175 g (6 oz) **ricotta** or **curd
   cheese**
½ teaspoon freshly grated
   nutmeg
1 teaspoon **salt**
1 quantity **3-egg Pasta
   Dough** (see page 10)
Italian 00 or **fine plain flour**,
   for dusting
125 g (4 oz) **butter**, melted
black pepper
freshly grated **Parmesan
   cheese**, to serve

Put the spinach and ricotta or curd cheese in a food processor with the nutmeg, salt and pepper to taste and process until smooth. Cover and refrigerate while you roll out the pasta dough.

Roll the pasta dough out into long sheets (see page 11). Working on one sheet at a time, add a heaped teaspoonful of filling every 5 cm (2 inches) until half the sheet is filled. Lightly brush with water and fold the empty side over the filling. Gently but firmly push down between the filling, sealing the pasta and ensuring that there is no trapped air. Cut into squares using a pastry wheel, crinkle cutter or a sharp knife, or cut into semicircles with an upturned glass. Transfer to a floured baking sheet and cover with a tea towel.

Cook the pasta in a large saucepan of salted boiling water for 2–3 minutes until al dente. Drain thoroughly, return to the pan and toss with the melted butter. Divide between 4 warmed serving plates and serve immediately with a scattering of grated Parmesan.

For sage & chilli butter, to dress the cooked ravioli, fry 12 sage leaves in the melted butter for 2 minutes, then stir in 3 tablespoons snipped chives and 1 deseeded and finely chopped mild green chilli.

pasta with pumpkin & sage

Serves **4**

Preparation time **30 minutes**

Cooking time **25 minutes**

250 g (8 oz) **pumpkin flesh**, cubed

1 **garlic clove**, crushed

2 **sage sprigs**

2 tablespoons **extra virgin olive oil**

75 g (3 oz) **ricotta cheese**

25 g (1 oz) **Parmesan cheese**, freshly grated, plus extra to serve

1 quantity **2-egg Pasta Dough** (see page 10)

Italian 00 or **fine plain flour**, for dusting

75 g (3 oz) **butter**

2 tablespoons whole **sage leaves**

salt and black pepper

lemon juice, to serve

Put the pumpkin in a small roasting tin with the garlic, sage sprigs and oil. Season with salt and pepper. Cover loosely with foil and roast in a preheated oven, 200°C (400°F), Gas Mark 6, for 20 minutes until soft. Transfer to a bowl, mash well and leave to cool.

Once cold, beat the ricotta and Parmesan into the pumpkin purée and season with salt and pepper to taste.

Roll the pasta dough out into thin sheets (see page 11). Cut into 8 cm (3¼ inch) squares. Place a spoonful of the filling in the centre of each. Brush the edges with water, then fold the dough over the filling to make triangles. Gently but firmly push down between the filling to seal, ensuring that there is no trapped air. Transfer to a floured baking sheet and cover with a tea towel.

Cook the pasta in a large saucepan of salted boiling water for 3–4 minutes until al dente. Meanwhile, melt the butter with the sage leaves and pepper until it just begins to turn a nutty brown colour. Drain the pasta and serve immediately bathed in the sage butter, with a squeeze of lemon juice and a scattering of grated Parmesan.

For almond & basil topping, make a sauce by frying 12 basil leaves and 50 g (2 oz) flaked almonds in 4 tablespoons olive oil until the basil crisps up. Spoon over the drained pasta and finish with lemon juice and Parmesan, as above.

index

acknowledgements

Executive editor: Nicky Hill
Editor: Fiona Robertson
Deputy creative director: Karen Sawyer
Designer: Cobalt
Photographer: Lis Parsons
Food stylist: Pippa Cuthbert
Prop stylist: Liz Hippisley
Production manager: Ian Paton

Special photography: © Octopus Publishing Group
Limited/Lis Parsons
Other photography: © Octopus Publishing Group
Limited 23, 186; /William Lingwood 102, 112, 116,
142, 204, 212; /Neil Marsh 74; /Lis Parsons 8, 13,
94, 106; /William Reavell 170; /William Shaw 76;
Simon Smith 11; /Ian Wallace 48, 80, 122, 150, 162,
166, 188, 198